THE ULTIMATE BOOK OF SCAVENGER HUNTS

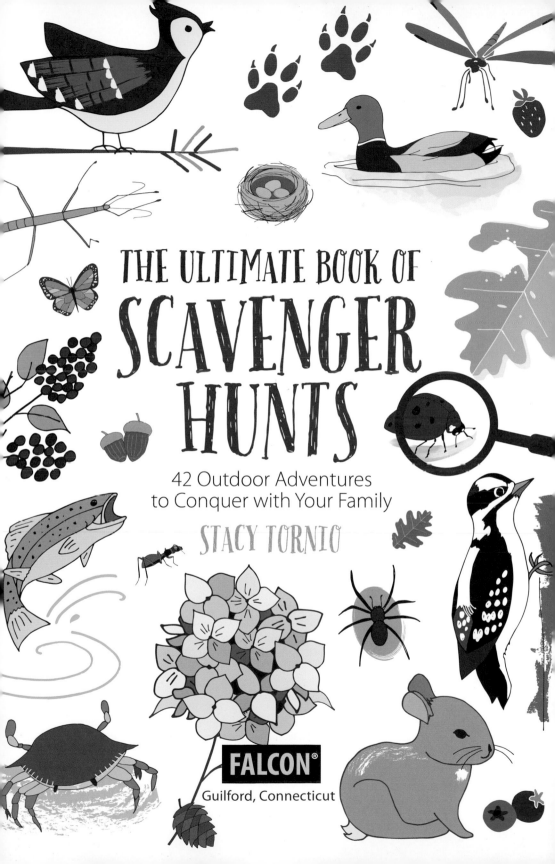

THE ULTIMATE BOOK OF
SCAVENGER
HUNTS

42 Outdoor Adventures to Conquer with Your Family

STACY TORNIO

FALCON®

Guilford, Connecticut

An imprint of The Rowman & Littlefield Publishing Group, Inc.
4501 Forbes Blvd., Ste. 200
Lanham, MD 20706
www.rowman.com
Falcon and FalconGuides are registered trademarks and Make Adventure Your Story
is a trademark of The Rowman & Littlefield Publishing Group, Inc.

Distributed by NATIONAL BOOK NETWORK

Illustrations by Corissa Nelson

British Library Cataloguing in Publication Information available

Library of Congress Cataloging-in-Publication Data

Names: Tornio, Stacy, author.
Title: The ultimate book of scavenger hunts : 42 outdoor adventures to conquer with
  your family / Stacy Tornio.
Description: Guilford, Connecticut : Falcon, [2020] | Summary: "Features forty-two
  scavenger hunts for children and families to participate in outdoors"—
  Provided by publisher.
Identifiers: LCCN 2019057366 (print) | LCCN 2019057367 (ebook) | ISBN
  9781493051533 (paperback) | ISBN 9781493051540 (epub)
Subjects: LCSH: Treasure hunt (Game) | Family recreation. | Outdoor recreation.
Classification: LCC GV1202.T7 T67 2020 (print) | LCC GV1202.T7 (ebook) |
  DDC 796.1/4—dc23
LC record available at https://lccn.loc.gov/2019057366
LC ebook record available at https://lccn.loc.gov/2019057367

♾™ The paper used in this publication meets the minimum requirements of American National Standard for Information Sciences—Permanence of Paper for Printed
Library Materials, ANSI/NISO Z39.48-1992.

I DEDICATE THIS BOOK
to a great mom, teacher, and friend—Andrea.
Thank you for all the years of support.

CONTENTS

CHAPTER 7: SEASONS 171

CHAPTER 8: GO AT THE RIGHT TIME 193

SPECIAL THANKS

I'd like to give a special thanks to my literary agent, Uwe Stender, who always hears me out and encourages me to try new things. I'd also like to thank my editor, Katie Benoit, who saw the vision for this book and helped make it better.

SOAP

INTRODUCTION

I s your family ready to explore the great outdoors? This big book of scavenger hunts is filled with activities to do and things to see when you're outside. With forty-two hunts and hundreds of items to find, this is a book that will keep your entire family busy for hours upon hours. Best of all—you won't need any batteries or electronics to complete any of the scavenger hunts. You just need to have a good eye and a love for going outside.

Use scavenger hunts to get kids interested in nature.
You probably already have a family that likes to go outside, but how much do you really explore and learn about your surroundings? These scavenger hunts provide a gateway to learning more about the natural world. Each item you find has fun facts or tidbits you can learn and read as you go. It'll help

you gain an understanding and appreciation of what you see. In turn, your entire family is going to learn a lot more about nature.

Scavenger hunts are great for any age.

The great thing about scavenger hunts is that you can do them at any age. It's not always about being "first" to see something and point it out to others. You can also turn a scavenger hunt into an individual or team challenge, working together or challenging each person to find the items. Pretty soon, everyone in the family will be pulled into the scavenger hunts, trying to get everything crossed off the list to make it complete.

From rural to urban, there are so many great things to see.

Do you live in the city? Do you live in the country? These scavenger hunts can really be done anywhere. Many of the items on the list can be found right in your own backyard or neighborhood. You might have to challenge yourself to take a walk or do some exploring, but there really are a lot of things you'll find where you currently live. Those things that require a special visit or trip can then be good adventures to have with your family. Take this book with you on a road trip or on a family vacation so that you always have something new to look for.

So are you ready to start exploring? It's time to start conquering all these scavenger hunts and learning about the awesome natural world we have around us. Let's go!

Chapter 1
SEARCH FOR ANIMALS

Do you love animals? There are so many great animals to see in the world around us, so this chapter is filled with scavenger hunts just for that. Many of the hunts will have you going to specific or special places to get all the items listed, so get ready for many great adventures with your family. Don't get discouraged if you don't cross off all the items on each hunt in one trip. It's just a reason to go back again, and again, and again. You might even want to do many of these scavenger hunts more than once!

AQUARIUM SCAVENGER HUNT

It can be challenging to see fish, dolphins, and other sea creatures up close, but not when you go to an aquarium! You can find aquariums both big and small all around the country, giving you the chance to look at some of those magical and mysterious animals for yourself. Take this scavenger hunt along with you, and see how many points you can rack up in a day.

NUMBER OF ITEMS: 12
TOTAL POINTS POSSIBLE: 24

☐ JELLYFISH

2 points
Here's a fun fact about jellyfish—they do not have a brain. These squishy sea creatures float around the water, looking for food. You probably won't see them eat, though. The mouth of a jellyfish is directly under its dome-shaped body. So it has to float over the food to eat it.

CRAB

1 point

A male crab is called a Jimmy and female crab is called a Sally. The local aquarium staff can probably help you learn how to tell a male from a female, but it has to do with the underside. When you see a crab in an aquarium, watch closely and you might notice that it's walking sideways. They really do go sideways—they'll even swim this way too.

SEA

2 points

While you're at the aquarium, challenge yourself to learn about the sea or ocean—there will be plenty of photos and fact displays around. You might even be lucky enough to visit an aquarium located near an ocean, where you might be able to see the waters from the inside. Look for signs that help you better understand these great waters and what kinds of animals you can find there. Then use the blank section at the end of this chapter to write down some of the cool facts you read.

☐ SHARK

2 points

You won't find any bones in sharks.
Some people think their fins are bones,
but they aren't—they're actually a type
of cartilage. Don't make the mistake of thinking sharks are
dangerous; most are not. Also, many aren't very big either.
Some are just a few feet long and look more like a regular fish
than what most people think of when they hear they're going
to see a shark.

☐ OCTOPUS

2 points

There are more than 250 types of
octopus, and they can range quite a bit
in size. In fact, the largest species, the
giant Pacific, grows to be more than
9 feet long and 600 pounds! Count all
eight tentacles on the octopus when you see it in the aquarium,
and then watch how it uses them. It's pretty amazing to watch
them in action.

☐ SEAHORSE

3 points

One of the coolest things about
seahorses is that the males have a little
pouch in their belly where the females
place the eggs. Then the male seahorse
carries them there until it's time for the

young to hatch. This is unique in the animal world. Another fun fact is that seahorses eat all the time and might consume more than 3,000 shrimp in a day.

☐ STINGRAY

2 points

Watch a stingray swim through the water and you'll see that they move very gracefully and gently. It's almost as if they are gliding through the water, which is a good thing because it helps them sneak up on their prey. If you're looking for a stingray at an aquarium, look low. Most of the time, stingrays like hanging along the bottom of the water.

☐ SEA TURTLE

2 points

There are seven different sea turtle species; sadly, most of them are on the endangered species list. These great turtles spend most of their time in the sea and then come to land to lay their eggs. These are some seriously old creatures—about 110 million years—that have been around since the dinosaurs. Learn about them at the aquarium and how you can help protect them. Being responsible on the beach and picking up after yourself are a start.

☐ STARFISH

1 point

Have you ever heard that starfish can regrow parts of their body? It's true! If they lose an arm, they can slowly regrow it over time. This is another animal with a lot of different types. There are more than 2,000 species of starfish in the world, and not all of them have five arms. Ask the aquarium workers how many different starfish are in their aquarium.

☐ CLOWN FISH

3 points

It's so much fun to see a real Nemo (clown fish) in person. You might think there's just one kind of clown fish, but there are actually more than thirty types. And not all are orange. A cool fact about these fish is that all are born as males, but some switch to become females as they get older. Yes, really!

☐ WALRUS

3 points

There is only one walrus species, but there are two subspecies—the Pacific and the Atlantic. They love cold weather and will use their two huge tusks to help chop holes in the ice. Walruses grow up to 11 feet long and 4,000 pounds. Males are usually twice the size of females.

☐ CORAL REEF

1 point

Coral reefs are so important to ocean life. Even though they cover less than 1 percent of the ocean, nearly 25 percent of all marine animals live in and around coral reefs. This is pretty amazing. Even if you don't see coral reefs in real life at the aquarium, look for signs or pictures with more information and cool facts.

**My Own Aquarium
Scavenger Hunt Checklist**

☐ _____

☐ _____

☐ _____

☐ _____

☐ _____

☐ _____

2 ZOO SCAVENGER HUNT

It's never a bad day to go to the zoo. You can spend hours wandering around from one habitat to the next. You'll find all sorts of amazing animals while also learning cool and interesting facts. Use this scavenger hunt to help you discover all the great areas of the zoo. You can find several different animals to meet each challenge on the list, so this is a scavenger hunt you can do again and again and again!

NUMBER OF ITEMS: 8
TOTAL POINTS POSSIBLE: 13

☐ ANIMAL WITH STRIPES

1 point

One of the most famous animals with stripes is the zebra, and no one is quite sure why zebras have stripes. Some think it's to confuse predators or offer some sort of camouflage. Others say the stripes could help repel insects or reduce body temperature.

☐ ANIMAL WITH SPOTS

2 points

Leopards are known for their spots, and there is a good explanation for why they have them. They do act as camouflage!

Like most animals that have spots (giraffes, cheetahs, some owls), this helps the leopard blend into its surroundings. This comes in handy when hunting.

☐ ANIMAL THAT LIVES IN AFRICA

1 point

You should be able to find a species of African animal in just about every exhibit at the zoo. So be sure to read about the animals you see and where they are from. You'll learn a lot. One of the most famous African animals is the elephant, which is the largest land animal on Earth. The second- and third-largest land animals—the rhino and the giraffe—are also found in Africa.

☐ ANIMAL THAT FLIES

1 point

You'll find plenty of options in the bird section of the zoo. But keep in mind that penguins won't count for this category— they can't fly. Try looking for a peacock instead. This is a very common zoo animal, and you'll see the males prancing around and making their beautiful feather display. Females of this bird family do not have the males' bright feathers and are called peahens.

☐ ANIMAL THAT LIVES IN THE GROUND

3 points

You'll definitely find animals in the small animal area that live in the ground. Gophers, rabbits, and skunks are just a few. Another burrowing animal that you might not think of is actually a bird. The burrowing owl has long legs and is the only owl in the world that lives underground. They use burrows that prairie dogs dig.

☐ ANIMAL THAT LIVES IN COLD WEATHER

1 point

The polar bear, walrus, and penguin are all great choices to look for in this category. A fun fact about polar bears is that they're not actually white. They have black skin, but their hair is hollow tubes (called guard hairs), which make them appear to be white. The dark skin helps them soak up the sun and stay warm.

☐ ANIMAL THAT LIVES IN TREES

2 points

Head on over to the monkey exhibit to knock this one off your list. Look for the chimpanzee, which is humans' closest living relative. They share about 98 percent of our genetic blueprint! Chimps like to live in groups, and in the wild can live to be forty to fifty years old.

☐ ANIMAL THAT IS NOCTURNAL
2 points

This is another one that you can knock off your list in a lot of different ways. You can find birds that are nocturnal (like owls) or other flying creatures (like bats). One nocturnal animal that you'll see at the zoo is the aardvark. Sometimes called antbears, they love to dig for ants and other bugs with their superlong snout.

My Own Zoo Scavenger Hunt Checklist

☐ _____

☐ _____

☐ _____

☐ _____

☐ _____

☐ _____

☐ _____

☐ _____

3 FARM SCAVENGER HUNT

The farm has so many things to do and see! Some things on this list are easy, and you'll spot them right away. But others will definitely be a challenge. You might even have to make a couple visits before you find all the items. Ready to head to the farm? Let's go!

NUMBER OF ITEMS: 12
TOTAL POINTS POSSIBLE: 23

☐ CHICKEN SCRATCHING

2 points

Chickens scratch at the ground because they are looking for bugs to eat. Bugs have a high level of protein in them, which is an important part of a chicken's diet. Sometimes you'll see chickens dig at a spot on the ground. This is likely because they know a bug is there, and they're working hard to get it out.

☐ COW MOOING

1 point

Cows moo because it's a form of communication; however, a moo can mean several different things. They might moo because they are telling another cow where they are. They might also moo because they are hungry or need to be milked. In most cases, cows are mooing because they have something to say.

☐ GOAT CLOMPING

3 points

All goats have a natural ability and interest in climbing. This includes both mountain goats and the small goats you see on farms. This is why you'll often see big ramps and structures in a farm's goat pens. It gives the goats room to climb, explore, and clomp around.

☐ PIG WALLOWING

3 points

Pigs love a good mud puddle, and there's a good reason why. Pigs don't have many sweat glands, so they get hot easily. Wallowing in mud and puddles cools off their bodies. Another reason pigs like to roll in the mud is that it gets them out of the sun.

☐ TRACTOR REVVING

1 point

Tractors on farms help farmers do so much. Most tractors have different attachments that allow them to do lots of different things. Some of these include mowing, digging, and planting. A lot of this work used to be done by plows, horses, and farmers, so tractors are a wonderful invention you'll find on just about every farm in the country.

☐ RED BARN

1 point

The most popular color for barns is red, but have you ever wondered why? It's because way back when, farmers used a lot of oil on their farms, which would create rust. Since rust is red, a lot of the

barns would get this color on them naturally. It must've stuck, because when paint was first developed in colors, farmers wanted to paint their barns red.

☐ CAT POUNCING

2 points

Many farmers have cats on the farm, and they call them barn cats. These barn cats have a job to do. Farmers are hoping the cats can keep their barns free of mice. Often you'll see two or three cats

in a barn because they like staying together. Plus, farmers know catching mice can be a big job, so you might need a couple of cats to help out.

☐ HORSE GALLOPING

1 point

Horses definitely gallop when they are being ridden, but they also gallop for other reasons. They might be playing with one another, or they might be fighting with another horse or trying to

protect their own space. Take some time to watch a group of horses and notice when they gallop.

☐ ROOSTER CROWING

3 points

Most roosters have what people call an internal clock. This is like a little alarm clock in their head, and it tells them what time of day it is. So just before the sun starts to rise, a rooster will often start crowing because its internal clock is saying it's almost time to start the day. Another reason roosters crow is to establish their territory. A rooster wants to send a message that this is its space and others shouldn't be nearby.

☐ FOOD GROWING

1 point

Most farms have a garden, growing food for the people that live on the farm. Of course the sole purpose of some farms is to grow big crops like potatoes, corn, and more. This is different than the farm's personal garden, which usually has several different things growing.

☐ DONKEY BRAYING

3 points

Why do donkeys bray? The reason for their funny *hee-haw* sound is similar to why cows moo. It's a form of communication. Sometimes they're trying to talk to the farmer, saying "I'm hungry!" For many donkeys, it is a way for them to announce themselves and claim their territory. It's like they're saying, "This is my spot!"

☐ DOG RELAXING

2 points

So many farms have dogs on them, and there are plenty of reasons why. First of all, they're just good, loyal companions for the farmer. They often go out early and late in the day as the farmer works or does his or her chores. Dogs sometimes have jobs on farms too. If there are animals, dogs might be used to help herd the animals and keep them in check.

My Own Farm Scavenger Hunt Checklist

☐ _____

☐ _____

☐ _____

☐ _____

☐ _____

☐ _____

☐ _____

☐ _____

☐ _____

4 BIRD WALK SCAVENGER HUNT

It's nice to go out for a walk or hike, but have you ever gone out with the purpose of looking for birds? If not, it's time! This scavenger hunt will really make you notice what's up in the trees and all around you. If you want to get a closer look at the birds you're going to see, be sure to grab some binoculars. You might also try doing your walk near a lake, pond, or stream—these are all great spots for birds. If you really want to know what you're seeing, check out a bird book or field guide at the local library. Then you can look up each one!

NUMBER OF ITEMS: 10
TOTAL POINTS POSSIBLE: 20

☐ BLUE JAY

3 points
Blue jays are mostly found in the central
and eastern parts of the United States.
But if you're in the West, you can also
count other jays (like the Steller's jay or California scrub-jay). Blue jays sometimes take ants and wipe them across their feathers; this is called anting. Why are they doing this? Scientists think they are getting rid of a secretion on the ant so they can digest them better.

☐ ROBIN

1 point

This is a very popular bird across the world. It's the state bird of Connecticut, Michigan, and Wisconsin, and it's even the national bird of Great Britain. Male robins have beautiful songs—try to learn to recognize it by first looking it up on YouTube. They are often some of the earliest and latest singers in the day.

☐ CHICKADEE

1 point

Many times you hear about birds moving around a lot or migrating from one area to another for food or nesting. Chickadees can move some, but for the most part, they are considered nonmigratory. This means they mostly stay in the same area throughout the year. So the chickadee you see in your backyard in spring might be the same one you see in fall or winter.

☐ HAWK

2 points

There are so many hawks you can find when you're out on a bird walk. The best place to find a hawk is up in a tree or perched out in the open where it's looking for something to eat. (They are pretty high up in the food chain, so they don't have to hide like

some birds.) The smallest hawk is the American kestrel, which weighs only 4 ounces. The largest is the ferruginous hawk, which can weigh more than 5 pounds. Female hawks are bigger than males!

☐ EAGLE

3 points

There are only four types of eagles in the whole world, and two of them are found in North America: the bald eagle and the golden eagle. They both build large nests that can be several feet wide and high. This can make them easier to spot up high in a tree or near a cliff. The largest golden eagle nest was 20 feet tall and 8 feet wide; the largest bald eagle nest weighed more than 2 tons!

☐ DUCK

2 points

There are so many duck species around the world. In fact, this is an animal you can find on every continent except Antarctica. The most common duck in North America is the mallard, but challenge yourself to look for other species as well. Your best chance to find ducks is to go near the water. Male ducks are called drakes, females are called hens, and baby ducks are called ducklings.

☐ MOURNING DOVE

1 point

This is a very common bird throughout North America. Often the sound of a mourning dove (*woo-woo-wooooo-wooo*) is mistaken for an owl. (Yes, it does kind of sound like a hoot! So don't let that fool you at night.) These birds like their seeds and sometimes gather up lots of seeds at a time to hide in an area of their throat called the crop. They keep them here and eat them later on.

☐ GOLDFINCH

2 points

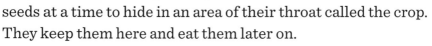

Goldfinches are beautiful birds, often with bright golden feathers. Well, actually, it's the males that have these bright feathers. The females are usually duller in color, more like a pale yellow or a yellow-green. And the males don't have these colorful feathers all the time. They go through a molt in the fall and become a dull shade for winter. During the cold months, you might not even recognize goldfinches at your feeder or in your backyard because they look so different.

☐ WOODPECKER

2 points

This is another one where there are so many different species to see. If you really want to challenge yourself, try to see three or four different types of woodpeckers in a single walk! Pretty much all woodpeckers have a very long tongue. Once they peck on wood and create a hole, they'll stick their tongue inside to reach the bugs.

☐ NUTHATCH

3 points

This is a pretty common bird to see at a backyard bird feeder, so if you know someone who feeds birds, you might want to stop by. If you're going on your bird walk at a nature center, there's a good chance you'll see a nuthatch. These birds have an awesome little habit of going up and down a tree headfirst, so a lot of people think of the nuthatch as the upside-down bird. It's pretty cool to see, and then you'll be able to recognize it right away. Once you do, you can be really far away but know immediately when you see a nuthatch.

My Own Bird Walk
Scavenger Hunt Checklist

☐ _____

☐ _____

☐ _____

☐ _____

☐ _____

☐ _____

5 BUGS & BUTTERFLIES SCAVENGER HUNT

Bugs and butterflies are all around us, but they often get missed because they're smaller and quicker than most animals. This scavenger hunt will put them front and center, so go out and see how many points you can rack up in a single afternoon. Here's a tip for finding butterflies: Go out in the heat of the day, because they're very active during this time. And for a tip on seeing bugs: Don't forget to look everywhere, not just in front of you. They can be on tree bark, low to the ground, under leaves, and elsewhere.

NUMBER OF ITEMS: 10
TOTAL POINTS POSSIBLE: 20

☐ LADYBUG

1 point

Ladybugs are also known as ladybirds or lady beetles. You can find this little bug all over the world—in fact, there are more than 5,000 different types, and they're not all red with black spots. Gardeners and farmers really like ladybugs because they eat a lot of aphids. Aphids often destroy gardens and crops, so the ladybug is helping a lot!

☐ MONARCH

3 points

The monarch butterfly is probably the most popular and recognized butterfly with its bold orange and black markings. There is a fun and easy way to tell if you're looking at a male monarch versus a female. Males have a dot on the lower part of each wing; females don't. Once you learn this little trick, you'll be able to recognize a male or female immediately.

☐ BEETLE

2 points

There are many species of beetles in the world. Scientists think there are probably more than 350,000 different beetles, and there are probably even more that haven't been discovered. Beetles go through a metamorphosis just like butterflies, so they go from egg to larva to pupa to adult.

☐ SWALLOWTAIL

2 points

There are a few different types of swallowtail butterflies, but all are larger butterflies with beautiful, bright colors. A fun fact about the swallowtail caterpillar is that it looks like bird droppings. This is a good thing—it helps keep predators away so that the caterpillar doesn't get eaten.

☐ GRASSHOPPER

1 point

Grasshoppers are definitely known for their hopping. They can reach distances more than twenty times the length of their body! Can you imagine if you could jump twenty times the height of you! Grasshoppers do not have ears on their head; they're on their belly instead.

☐ AZURE

3 points

This one might be challenging, but it's definitely worth it if you can spot a spring azure butterfly. These little blue butterflies are only about 1 inch wide, so start looking for something small. Keep in mind that their blue coloring is more prominent when they have their wings open instead of closed. When they are perched with their wings closed, they look gray overall. This little butterfly will likely stop in gardens all across North America.

☐ ANT

1 point

This is another bug with many different types. There are more than 12,000 different ant species in the world. They might be small, but they can do some pretty impressive things. Ants are considered one of the strongest bugs around. They can carry up to fifty times their weight; they'll even get together as a group to move larger objects back to their nest or anthill.

☐ SULPHUR

3 points

The most common sulphur butterfly is the cloudless sulphur, a species you can find throughout North America. These pretty yellow butterflies are fairly easy to spot once you know what you're looking for. Like many butterflies, they like to do something called puddling, where they gather around a mud puddle to have a drink and get some nutrients. Many butterfly species do this, especially if it's been raining lately.

☐ FLY

1 point

The most common fly is the housefly you see buzzing around picnics or food area. Just like butterflies, houseflies can taste with their feet. They also have a complete liquid diet, so when  they do land on a food area, they're just sucking up the juices of whatever they can find. Flies usually have a pretty short life span of just a couple weeks to thirty days.

☐ SKIPPER

3 points

This is another butterfly that tends to be on the smaller side. There are lots of different skippers around the world and in North America, and in general  they range in size from 1 to 3 inches. One thing that almost all skippers have in common is the way they fly. They are quick and can be kind of jerky in movement from one spot to the next. This jerkiness is a great thing to look for when you're trying to find a skipper.

My Own Bugs & Butterflies
Scavenger Hunt Checklist

☐ _____

☐ _____

☐ _____

☐ _____

☐ _____

☐ _____

☐ _____

☐ _____

☐ _____

Chapter 2
CHECK OUT THE NEIGHBORHOOD

Are you ready to explore right in your own backyard? This chapter has so many items to find because there are so many great things right where you are. Yep—you don't have to travel great distances or go to really special places to have a cool scavenger hunt. Many of these can be done within a few miles from where you live. Some you might even be able to walk or bike to, depending on what kind of area you live in. Be sure to add lots of items to the blank pages—it'll really help make these scavenger hunts unique and specific to your area.

6 FARMERS' MARKET SCAVENGER HUNT

The farmers' market is a happy place. It's filled with homemade good, fresh veggies, and friendly farmers. The people at a farmers' market take so much pride in their work, and they're usually really willing to talk to you, tell you about what they're selling, and even give tips. If you're going to the market, don't forget to take along your own bag to cut down on the use of plastic.

NUMBER OF ITEMS: 10
TOTAL POINTS POSSIBLE: 19

☐ SUNFLOWERS

1 point

The sunflower is one of the few blooms with the word "flower" in its name. (Now you're trying to think of others, aren't you? *Psst*—monkey flower!) Sunflowers are a popular flower, and they make a great cut flower. You can find many different varieties of sunflowers, ranging from mini sunflowers (1 to 2 feet tall) to large ones that can grow more than 6 feet high.

☐ STRAWBERRIES

1 point

California is one of the largest producers of strawberries in the world. In fact, more than 1 billion strawberries come from California each year! This might be one of the most popular spring fruits, and they are very good for you too. They are an excellent source of vitamin C and antioxidants.

☐ FRESH-BAKED BREAD

2 points

Fresh-baked break is a very popular market item in Europe, and it's a great item to look for at farmers' markets. On average in America, people consume about 53 pounds of bread each year. If you can use that bread to serve up some freshly made bruschetta, you'll definitely be enjoying the farmers' market to the fullest.

☐ CORN

2 points

Most countries actually refer to corn as maize. Have you ever thought about how many kernels there are on an individual piece of corn? Of course it can vary, but many cobs of corn have sixteen rows of corn and about 800 individual kernels. Count the rows on the next ear of corn you have. Are there sixteen?

☐ ONIONS

1 point

Onions are one of the oldest veggies in the world. In ancient Egypt, onions were thought to be a sign of eternal life. In Europe, newlyweds would eat onions the morning after their wedding night.

If you've tried onions but don't like them, try a different type. There are a lot of options, and some are a lot sweeter in flavor. Ask one of the local vendors at the farmers' market for a recommendation.

☐ HANDMADE SOAP

3 points

A lot of times, soap you buy at the store can dry your hands out. Many handmade soaps contain natural oils and other plant-based ingredients. This soap is often better for your hands and will keep them softer.

☐ JELLY

2 points

Do you know the difference between jam and jelly? Most of the time, jelly is made from the juice of the fruit. You strain the fruit to create a very smooth final product. Jam has more fruit pieces in it, so it tends to be thicker and chunkier.

☐ FARM-FRESH EGGS

3 points

The eggs you buy in the store are often four to six months old from the time the chickens first laid them. When you buy eggs at the farmers' market, you are getting much fresher eggs. Another good

comparison between a farm-fresh egg and a store egg is the yolk. Look at it yourself and you'll see. Farm eggs tend to have a yolk that is creamier and richer in color. Many say it tastes better too!

☐ HONEY

2 points

Bees are pretty impressive insects. To make 1 pound of honey, the bees of a colony need to collect nectar from about 2 million flowers. It depends on the size of the hive, but a good, healthy group of bees from a single hive can make about 30 to 100 pounds of honey a year. Another fun fact is that honey is one of the few foods that never spoil!

☐ SALSA

2 points

If you go to a farmers' market that offers homemade salsa, you are definitely at a good location! Plus, there's a good chance they'll have some samples. While there is the traditional tomato salsa in mild, medium, and hot, branch  out and taste some other flavors as well. For instance, salsa verde is made with tomatillos. You can also try a pineapple or mango salsa for a fruity flavor.

My Own Farmers' Market Scavenger Hunt Checklist

- ☐ _____
- ☐ _____
- ☐ _____
- ☐ _____
- ☐ _____
- ☐ _____
- ☐ _____
- ☐ _____

PARK SCAVENGER HUNT

1

This is a scavenger hunt you can do again and again at different parks. Most of these things should be at your local park, but it might take you a little time or effort to find them all. Don't forget to fill out your own list at the end to really personalize your park experience. You know your area best, and that will make it really fun.

NUMBER OF ITEMS: 8
TOTAL POINTS POSSIBLE: 15

☐ ONE SPIDERWEB

2 points

All spiders can produce silk, but not all spiders spin webs. The spiders that do spin webs have glands on their abdomens called spinnerets. The web material (silk) that comes out is a liquid at first, but it dries to become strong and sturdy webs. While the orb shape is the spiderweb that most people think of, spiders spin webs in all different sizes and shapes.

☐ TWO NESTS

3 points

What's the best way to find a bird's nest? This can be a challenge, but there are a couple of different strategies you can use. First, you can just look in the trees. It's best to be a little bit away from the tree (instead of right up next to it). Then look for any groupings of twigs, leaves, or little mounds that might be a nest. The second way to find a nest is to watch for birds to fly there. Keep in mind that it needs to be nesting season (spring or early summer) to watch for birds to go to their nests. But this is a really good way to find a nest.

☐ THREE DOGS

1 point

Have you ever thought about a dog's nose and just how powerful it is? Humans have about 6 million olfactory receptors in their nose; by comparison, dogs have 300 million! The part of the brain that is dedicated to analyzing smells is also bigger for dogs—about forty times larger than in a human. So when you see a dog out and about, be impressed by how powerful its sniffer is.

☐ FOUR BUTTERFLIES

3 points

Butterflies like hot temperatures. In fact, they can't fly if their body temperature is less than 86°F. So if you happen to come across a butterfly that is perched and not moving, just leave it alone. It might just be waiting for the temperatures to heat up. Another reason a butterfly might be perched is that it just came out of its chrysalis and is waiting to dry before it takes off for the first flight.

☐ FIVE BIRDS

1 point

To see lots of butterflies, you definitely want to go out in the hot part of the day, but this is not the case for birds. The best time to see birds is early. But no matter what time of day you're out, be sure to use your ears when looking for birds too. Listen to where their tweets, twerps, and songs are coming from. Then follow the sound in hopes of a sighting.

☐ SIX SQUIRRELS

2 points

Here are a couple of fun facts about squirrels. First, their front two teeth never stop growing. They will gnaw them down throughout their life to keep them at the right length. Another fun fact is that squirrels will sometimes pretend to bury a nut (even though they don't have one) to throw off a potential food thief.

☐ SEVEN LADYBUGS

2 points

What do ladybugs do in the wintertime?
A lot of them go into hibernation! Yes,
ladybugs do hibernate when it gets cold
outside. They will find a warm and safe
place to stay in winter, like the inside of a log. They will emerge
when it warms back up.

☐ EIGHT PINECONES

1 point

While all conifer trees and shrubs
produce cones, only pine trees produce
pinecones. When it's cold outside, these
cones will close up to protect the seeds
inside. But then it heats up, they open
again. See if you can notice this on warm and cold days. It really
is cool to see the difference.

My Own Park Scavenger Hunt Checklist

☐ _____

☐ _____

☐ _____

☐ _____

☐ _____

NATURE TRAIL SCAVENGER HUNT

It's time to hit the trail. This scavenger hunt will take you on a little walk or hike at your favorite natural place. And you should get bonus points if you go to a national park, state park, or wildlife refuge. This is another one that you can do over and over again, especially if you go to new or different nature trails.

NUMBER OF ITEMS: 8
TOTAL POINTS POSSIBLE: 15

☐ GRASS TALLER THAN YOU

3 points

Not all nature trails are going to have this one. Your best bet is to look for places that have prairies or other areas they're letting go wild (instead of mowing). This is so beneficial for insects, birds, and other animals. When you do find grass growing taller than you, be sure to get a picture. You'll want photo proof!

☐ TREE WITH BERRIES

2 points

Trees with berries are a popular option for your backyard if you're trying to attract birds, and if you look closely, you should be able to find trees with berries just about any time of the year. Yes, even in winter some conifers will have

berries. You might have to look closely in some cases, because the berries can be hidden or tucked away.

☐ WHITE FLOWERS

1 point

This should be an easy one because white is a common color for flowers. Whether you look for the traditional daisy or something like hydrangeas, challenge yourself to find the biggest

and the smallest white flower you can. If you can identify it, you should get another point!

☐ BENCH

2 points

Every good nature center or trail will have benches along the way. It's even better if they are at an overlook where you can sit and observe all the great things around you. An Aldo Leopold

bench has a very distinct look, like you see in the illustration here. If you find one, give yourself an extra point.

☐ WATER FLOWING

2 points

Along your walk, look (and listen) for a source of water. If you're near a lake or pond, that doesn't count. The water needs to be flowing. So look for a waterfall, river, or even just a stream

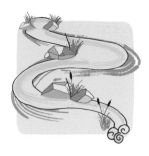

flowing to the bigger body of water. It has to be in motion for this scavenger hunt item to count.

☐ BIKER BIKING

2 points

Many nature centers or trails share their space with walkers, hikers, and bikers. The biking area might be separate from the hiking area, or it could be all together. Look for mountain bikes

(bigger tires) on dirt and wooded paths and road bikes (skinny, smooth tires) on paved areas.

☐ MAP

1 point

Do you know where you're going? How far? Which direction? Look for a map around the nature trail to help you out with this one. It can take a little bit of practice to learn how to read and follow

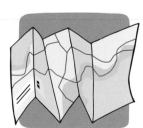

a map. Take the time to learn. It's a great skill to have for the future too.

☐ GRASSHOPPERS

2 points

Are you able to hear a grasshopper
before you see it? Many grasshoppers
make a noise by rubbing their back legs
against their forewings or body. They
can also make a noise with their wings
when they fly. It's almost like a snapping sound as they take off
from one place to the next.

My Own Nature Trail
Scavenger Hunt Checklist

☐ _____

☐ _____

☐ _____

☐ _____

☐ _____

☐ _____

☐ _____

☐ _____

9 LAKE, POND, OR RIVER SCAVENGER HUNT

There is something therapeutic about being around water. It makes people happy. It's soothing. It's beautiful. Whether you have a favorite spot to walk or you find a totally new-to-you place, there is so much life around the water. Take a look at a few of the things you might see.

NUMBER OF ITEMS: 8
TOTAL POINTS POSSIBLE: 14

☐ FISH JUMPING

3 points

You can often hear the splash of a fish after it jumps through the air, but it's an even bigger challenge to actually see it for yourself. Why exactly do fish jump?

There are some various opinions on this, but most agree that it's one of two reasons. First, they're trying to get away from something, like a predator. Second, they're trying to reach something, like an insect.

☐ DRAGONFLY FLYING

2 points

Did you know that a group of dragonflies is called a swarm? Dragonflies spend a lot of time around water. Some of the animals that eat dragonflies include birds, water beetles, and fish. So that fish you saw jumping (did you see it?) could've been after a dragonfly!

☐ BIRD SWOOPING

1 point

Let's keep talking about animals looking for food. That's because this is a big reason you'll see birds swooping around water. You might see tree swallows (or other birds) swooping up, down, and all around as they look for insects to eat. You might also see a bird like a kingfisher or eagle, swooping down to pull a fish out of the water.

☐ TURTLE SUNNING

2 points

Turtles are reptiles, so they need a lot of sunshine. They need UVB light, which produces vitamins that help them build calcium and other nutrients in their bodies. Remember this the next time you find turtles sunning themselves along a log. Often they'll even line up, one after another, to soak up the rays. You might even spot a young one perched on top of another. See who can see the most turtles on a really nice, sunny day!

☐ BIRD RESTING

1 point

Look up in those trees surrounding the water. Birds can be easy to miss, but they are probably there, watching patiently for a fish, insect, or something else to eat. Look for eagles, hawks, and kingfishers waiting to swoop down for a fish. Look for swallow and other birds hanging out for insects.

☐ LILY PAD FLOATING

1 point

It might seem like a lily pad is just magically floating on top of the water, but there is actually a stem attached. Lily pads have rhizomes that can grow a long stem (10 feet or more) that supports the pad on top of the water.

☐ MUSKRAT OR OTTER SWIMMING

3 points

Muskrats are actually rodents, so they are closely related to mice! They spend a lot of time in the water and can grow up to 25 inches long. Their tails can add another 8 to 10 inches! They like to build their homes near water and in the sides of riverbanks so they always have close access to the water.

☐ FISHERMAN OR FISHERWOMAN FISHING

1 point

Fishing is a popular hobby. Just how popular is it? One study estimates that about 1 million people spend an average of seventeen days fishing each year. If you want to talk fishing but don't want to say fisherman or fisherwoman, just say angler. This is a word for someone who fishes, without assigning a gender!

My Own Lake, Pond, or River
Scavenger Hunt Checklist

☐ _____

☐ _____

☐ _____

☐ _____

☐ _____

☐ _____

☐ _____

☐ _____

☐ _____

Chapter 3
HAVE A BACKYARD ADVENTURE

Step outside and start searching. This chapter focuses on great adventures you can have without going too far. From low to high, there are plenty of great things to find in your own backyard. All you have to do is look. So the next time you think, "I'm bored," pull out this chapter and go see what you can find!

10 SKY SCAVENGER HUNT

It's one of those beautiful days with sunshine, puffy clouds, and a soft breeze—a perfect time to lie outside on a blanket and watch the clouds roll by. Now let's look up and see what you can spot in those clouds. Can you find all the items in this list? You might have a friendly little contest with someone and see who can find the best-looking cloud of each item.

NUMBER OF ITEMS: 12
TOTAL POINTS POSSIBLE: 22

☐ DRAGON JUMPING

3 points

Are they good? Are they bad? Dragons are mythical creatures that have been in stories for hundreds if not thousands of years. In Japanese and Chinese cultures, they are definitely a sign of good. Plus, having a dragon's tooth is a symbol of good luck. In many other stories and cultures, they are often seen as evil. There are lots of challenges to "slay the dragon" in storybooks and myths. What do you think about dragons?

☐ ROCKET SOARING

1 point

Rockets are incredible, and it's really fun to watch one take off. Do you know how long it takes a rocket to reach the Moon? It's about 240,000 miles between the Earth and the Moon, and a typical rocket needs about three days to get there.

☐ LADYBUG CRAWLING

1 point

Ladybugs have a crafty way to keep predators away. They steal a trick from opossums and play dead. If you come across a ladybug that is as still as can be, keep watching it. It might just be playing dead and will soon start moving.

☐ SNAKE SLITHERING

1 point

Snakes slither to get to where they need to go, but did you know they might also be slithering to get out of their skin? Snakes typically shed their skin two to four times in a single year! Young snakes that are growing might shed a lot more frequently than that—even every couple of weeks as they're growing into their new skin. It's fun to look for a snake skin when you're on a hike.

☐ DUCK FLYING

2 points

You might not think that ducks are all that fast because you usually only see them taking off or landing. But they can actually be really fast. For instance, the mallard duck (the most common) usually flies at speeds of 40 to 60 miles per hour. They can travel several hundred miles in a single day!

☐ DINOSAUR WALKING

3 points

How well do you know your dinosaur facts? Scientist believe dinosaurs were on the Earth for more than 165 million years. They became extinct during a time called the Cretaceous period, about 65 million years ago. We know there were more than 700 different species, but even more could be discovered in the future.

☐ SPACESHIP FLOATING

3 points

Many people think of a spaceship as a kind of flat round object that aliens could come out of. But a spaceship can also look a lot like a rocket, because it's going up in space. Whatever you look for, good luck. This will be one of the toughest items to conquer.

☐ ELEPHANT EXPLORING

2 points

Do you know the three types of elephants that exist in the world? They are the African savanna, African forest, and Asian elephant. Elephants are the world's largest land animal. The African species can reach 7,500 pounds; the Asian ones are slightly smaller, getting up to 6,000 pounds.

☐ WAVES CRASHING

1 point

It might seem like waves are coming from the ocean, but it's actually the wind moving across the surface of the water. Waves transfer energy, not matter. So on windy days, you'll see waves that are much bigger and stronger.

☐ DOLPHIN SPLASHING

2 points

Yes, dolphins are known for splashing and jumping. Did you know they can jump 15 or more feet high? Here are a few additional facts about dolphins: Female dolphins are called cows, males are called bulls, and young dolphins are called calves.

☐ TORNADO SPINNING

2 points

Tornadoes have unique funnel shapes, and they have whirling winds that can reach up to 300 miles per hour. Did you know that "Tornado Alley" is a region of the United States where tornadoes are especially common? This includes areas of Texas, Oklahoma, Kansas, Nebraska, Colorado, and South Dakota.

☐ HEART BEATING

1 point

Your heart is a very important part of your body. Every day, your heart beats about 115,000 times. This means it will pump about 2,000 gallons of blood through your body. Remember this is every single day—pretty impressive!

My Own Sky Scavenger Hunt Checklist

☐ _____

☐ _____

☐ _____

☐ _____

☐ _____

11 HIGH & LOW SCAVENGER HUNT

Look up. Look down. Look all around. Sometimes we get so focused on just what's straight ahead that we forget to look up and down. This scavenger hunt will definitely break you out of that habit. You're about to see so many cool things. You just have to look.

NUMBER OF ITEMS: 8
TOTAL POINTS POSSIBLE: 16

☐ BIRD'S NEST HIGH IN THE TREES

2 points

When you're looking up high in trees for a bird's nest, don't be fooled by a squirrel's nest. Squirrels build big and messy nests, but most birds build smaller, compact nests.

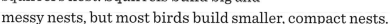

☐ BIRD'S NEST LOW IN THE SHRUBS

1 point

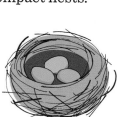

Birds like to hide their nests and really tuck them deep into the branches of a tree or shrub. Try not to move the branches too much, but do get up close and look into a shrub or branch to see if you can find a nest. For instance, a hummingbird's nest isn't much bigger than a quarter, so you have to look closely.

☐ BIRD SOARING IN THE SKY

2 points

You know those birds that soar in the sky really gently and slowly? It's like they're just letting the wind carry them wherever they want to go. They are often turkey vultures. They just kind of float in the sky as they look for food along roadsides and fields before swooping down to eat.

☐ ANIMAL HOME IN THE GROUND

3 points

It's not always easy to find an animal's home in the ground. The two most common animals with homes in the ground are foxes and rabbits, and you really have to look because the animals like to hide their entrances. Look for a little rise in the ground and see if you can find a hole in one side. Moles, voles, and snakes also live in the ground, often just in a hole. If you do find an animal home, be sure to give the animal some space. Remember that it's a home down there—you don't want to crowd it.

☐ LIGHTHOUSE

2 points

The United States has more lighthouses than any other country, and Michigan is the state with the most lighthouses. Michigan has more than 115 lighthouses on the Great Lakes that surround it.

☐ ANTS MARCHING

1 point

Have you ever heard the word "pheromone"? This is a scent that animals leave behind, and it is one of the reasons you see ants marching in a row.

They are leaving behind a pheromone when they walk, so the next ant falls in line and follows the scent. Some entomologists (scientists who study insects) call this a trail pheromone.

☐ RAINBOW

3 points

Do you know when to look for rainbows? Definitely after it rains, but you should always keep an eye out for them after mist, dew, and fog too. The seven colors of a rainbow are red, orange, yellow, green, blue, indigo, and violet.

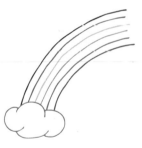

☐ PUDDLES

2 points

A puddle can be a very popular spot for animals—especially small ones. For instance, insects like bees, dragonflies, and butterflies will gather at puddles to drink or even get nutrients from the mud. If you see a puddle, take an even closer look for insects and other animals.

My Own High & Low Scavenger Hunt Checklist

☐ _____

☐ _____

☐ _____

☐ _____

☐ _____

☐ _____

☐ _____

☐ _____

12 OPPOSITES SCAVENGER HUNT

This is another scavenger hunt where you need to look for two things at once. You will want to look for items that are opposites! You can team up with friends to split the list or make it a challenge and have teams. This opposites hunt will really get you noticing the differences (and similarities) of items in nature.

NUMBER OF ITEMS: 6
TOTAL POINTS POSSIBLE: 12

☐ BIG ANIMAL AND LITTLE ANIMAL

2 points
What's counts as big or little? For this scavenger hunt item, you should try to find the biggest and smallest animal possible. This is another good one to have a challenge with your family members or friends. Or work as a team! What's can you discover together? (This is a good one to do at the zoo as well.)

☐ TALL TREE AND SHORT TREE

1 point

This is one where you could definitely use some photo evidence. Try to find the tallest tree possible and take a picture while you're standing next to it. Then look for a short tree and take another picture. Compare the two, and then try to identify them.

☐ LIGHT FLOWER AND DARK FLOWER

2 points

The easiest two flowers to find would be white and black, because they are on the opposite ends of the color spectrum, but true black flowers are rare. Any light or dark flower will do. You could even focus on a single color and try to find a light pink flower and then a dark pink flower.

☐ STRAIGHT LEAF AND CURLY LEAF

2 points

Leaves are so incredibly cool and different. It really seems that no two are alike. For this challenge, try to find two very different types of leaves. Go look for a really big, straight leaf. Then go find a smaller, curly leaf. Remember that leaves aren't just on trees. Try to find very different leaves, and then get a picture too!

☐ SLOW BUG AND FAST BUG

3 points

This one is definitely the most
challenging on the list. Look for a fast
bug, and then look for a slow bug. What
does fast or slow mean? It's a bit hard to
explain, but you'll know when you see it.
If you can find a slow and fast bug in the same space, you should
get a bonus point!

☐ WIDE ROCK AND NARROW ROCK

2 points

This one will be a lot easier than the
last one, but still challenge yourself to
find really cool and interesting rocks. If
you find two really cool rocks that are
different in size, stack them to show the differences.

My Own Opposites Scavenger Hunt Checklist

☐ _____

☐ _____

☐ _____

☐ _____

☐ _____

13 ROUND SCAVENGER HUNT

Shapes are all around us, and they're definitely in nature. For this scavenger hunt, it's all about round objects! You might not be able to knock this one out all in one spot or day, but don't give up. Keep looking for all of these items until you have everything checked off the list. While you're at it, add your own items to your own list at the end.

NUMBER OF ITEMS: 8
TOTAL POINTS POSSIBLE: 15

☐ APPLE

1 point

You might know a few types of apples, but did you know there are more than 2,500 different varieties in the United States? There are also more than 7,500 around the world! Commercially (what you find mostly in stores), there are only about 100 varieties, but that's still pretty impressive. What's your favorite apple?

☐ FULL MOON

3 points

The full moon isn't that difficult to catch, but you do need to do a little bit of work to make sure you see it. First, find out when the full moon will be by visiting a website like space.com or timeanddate.com. Then set up a plan to see and experience it.

☐ ACORN

2 points

You probably don't think of an acorn as being a piece of fruit, but it is the fruit of an oak tree. To find an acorn, you need to go where oak trees are. Many animals feed on this fruit, including birds, mice, squirrels, and deer. Sometimes it takes oak trees twenty years or more to start producing acorns.

☐ ONION

1 point

Do onions really make you cry? The answer is yes! They produce a chemical irritant that is hard on the eyes. If you want to avoid crying, try peeling the onion under cold water. This is usually enough to wash away the irritant so it doesn't get in the air and reach your eyes.

☐ SEA URCHIN

3 points

To see a live sea urchin, check out the tide pools along the ocean or beach. You might also be able to spot them in shallow water. If you look closely, you'll notice that this little animal is covered with little spines for protection. When the animal inside dies, the outer part might wash up on the shore, and you could find the shell.

☐ RABBIT POOP

2 points

This fact might gross you out a bit, but it's also cool. Rabbits sometimes eat parts of their poop. It can have important nutrients in it, so they eat it to help them be healthier. By the way, other words for poop include "feces" and "scat."

☐ CENTER OF A FLOWER

1 point

The center of a flower can be so different from one to the next, but for this scavenger hunt item, try to find one that has a nice round center. This part of the flower can often be a food source for animals. It can be a nectar source for butterflies or hummingbirds. It can also be a source of seed.

☐ WATER RIPPLES

2 points

Have you ever walked up to a perfectly still body of water where there's almost no movement happening? This is what you want for this scavenger hunt item. You want to find this still body of water and then toss a single rock into a clear area. If it's really calm and quiet, you should see a circle emerge from the surface.

My Own Round Scavenger Hunt Checklist

- ☐ _____
- ☐ _____
- ☐ _____
- ☐ _____
- ☐ _____
- ☐ _____
- ☐ _____
- ☐ _____
- ☐ _____

14 FLUFFY SCAVENGER HUNT

This fluffy scavenger hunt seeks out some of the softest, fluffiest items in nature. From little animal fluffs to fluff that comes from plants, there's a little bit of everything on this list. Not all items are ones you should touch. But for the ones you can—definitely give them a feel and enjoy the sensation on your skin.

NUMBER OF ITEMS: 7
TOTAL POINTS POSSIBLE: 13

☐ FOX

3 points
The red fox is most common fox in the United States. The gray fox is also fairly common in North America. It has unique claws and can climb trees almost like a cat! The smallest fox in the world is the fennec fox. It lives in Africa and is only about 9 to 16 inches long.

☐ BUNNY

1 point
When rabbits are born, their eyes are closed and they don't have any fur. These babies are also called kits or

kittens, and they grow up quickly. Soon they'll have that fluffy signature bunny tail. Even though rabbits are found around the world, about half of all rabbits live in North America.

☐ TREE FLUFF
2 points

Although there are multiple trees that can give off fluffy material, the most common is the cottonwood. This is a type of poplar tree, and the cotton-like seeds start shedding in summer and sometimes collect in big fluffy patches on the ground. Many people are allergic to this fluff, so if you notice this in your area and have a lot of sneezing going on, you might be allergic to it too.

☐ CLOUDS
1 point

Clouds are beautiful, especially on a blue-sky kind of day, but what are clouds exactly? Clouds forms when water evaporates from the earth. This water then gathers in the sky to create the white wispy things we think of as clouds. The most common types of clouds are stratus, cumulus, and cirrus. Those big puffy ones you see in the sky are cumulus.

☐ SHEEP

2 points

You know wool comes from sheep, right?
Well, wool is a pretty amazing thing.
One reason is because it grows forever.
Yes, as you keep shearing or trimming
a sheep, it will keep producing wool. A
little can go a long way too. In fact, about
1 pound of wool can make up to 10 miles of yarn!

☐ DANDELION

1 point

So many people dislike dandelions and
want to remove them from their yard
and garden, but did you know they are
actually beneficial in a lot of ways? They
are! All parts of the flower can be used

for important things like medicine and dye. Also, dandelions
are an important food source for many birds and insects. As
dandelions go to seed and turn from yellow flowers to puffy
white fluffs, they are perfect for picking and making a wish.

☐ CATTAIL

3 points

To see this one, you'll have to go to a pond or other wetland area. Like dandelions, many people think of cattails as a weed. But they also have a lot of positive benefits and are a good food source for birds and insects. These cool plants can grow up to 10 feet tall, and you'll often see little bits of fuzz breaking off from the main plant and floating through the air.

My Own Fluffy Scavenger Hunt Checklist

☐ _____

☐ _____

☐ _____

☐ _____

☐ _____

☐ _____

☐ _____

☐ _____

☐ _____

15 TINY SCAVENGER HUNT

You're going to have to really hunt for some of the items on this list. There are several challenging items, and it might take you a little time to get them all. Each one is filled with interest and awe, though. As you find each one, take the time to really admire and appreciate it.

NUMBER OF ITEMS: 8
TOTAL POINTS POSSIBLE: 18

SEED

1 point

It's not hard to find a seed on certain flowers, but it can be a lot more difficult on others. Take sunflowers for instance—those seeds are big and right there out in the open. Other seeds are hidden within a flower and aren't visible right away. You might even have to take a plant apart to find the seeds. If you want to gather seeds from a flower, snip off a bloom, put it in a paper bag, and hang it upside down. As the flower dries, the seeds will often fall out.

☐ DEWDROP

2 points

Why do dewdrops form? The air can only hold a certain amount of water, so when it's full, little drops will gather on surrounding surfaces. It's common to see dewdrops when it's hot and humid outside. And if you go out early in the morning, dew can give you a pretty awesome photo opportunity.

☐ HUMMINGBIRD

3 points

Hummingbirds are amazing and oh so tiny. The birds themselves are only a few inches in length, depending on the species. Hummingbird eggs are about the size of a Tic Tac! Now combine the hummingbird's small size with the fact that it moves really fast (about 50 miles per hour), and it's no surprise that it can be difficult to spot this really cool little bird.

☐ POLLEN

2 points

Do you know your parts of a flower? The stamen is where the pollen is produced. Take a very close look at a flower, and try to fine the yellow pollen on the stamen. You might also see pollen sticking to the feet of a bee as it goes from one flower

to the next. Pollen has a very important job. It helps with the reproduction process of flowers. Pollen travels from one flower to the next (either by the wind or with the help of insects) to keep the species growing and reproducing.

☐ BABY BIRD

3 points

It's a myth that if you touch a baby bird the mother bird will abandon it. That doesn't mean you should touch a baby bird. However, if you happen to find a baby bird that has fallen out of its nest,

it is okay to put it back in. The mom isn't going to leave.

☐ OWL PELLET

3 points

If you've never seen an owl pellet, google it. This will help you know what you're looking for. (It kind of looks like a piece of poop!) A pellet is undigested parts of an owl's food. The owl coughs it back up

in this neat little pellet. If you find one, feel free to dissect it. It might sound kind of gross, but it's actually pretty cool.

☐ SPIDER

1 point

Spiders are not insects. They are in their own class of arachnids because they have two body segments instead of three like insects. Many people don't like spiders, but they really are good. In fact, if you leave the spiders you see in and around your home alone, they will eat most of the bad bugs!

☐ SNAIL

3 points

What's the difference between a snail and a slug? Nothing! They are pretty much the same thing, except snails have a shell. There are thousands of different types of snails around the world, and one species can grow to be more than 1 foot long!

My Own Tiny Scavenger Hunt Checklist

☐ _____

☐ _____

☐ _____

☐ _____

☐ _____

Chapter 4
EXPLORE THE WILD

Are you feeling adventurous? The scavenger hunts in this chapter will get you out to explore some of those paths that are a little less traveled by most people. The places might be a little harder to get to, but the things you see will definitely be worth the extra effort. This is where you'll start to see wild animals, rare nature moments, and lots of beautiful sights. Be sure to have good walking shoes and a camera to capture all those great moments.

16 HIKING SCAVENGER HUNT

When you go out for a walk in or around the woods, there are always plenty of cool sights to see in nature. There's something peaceful about getting away from the busyness of a city or even a neighborhood to really take in all the cool natural elements around you. Here are a few of those things to look for when you're out on your hike.

NUMBER OF ITEMS: 10
TOTAL POINTS POSSIBLE: 18

☐ WOODEN SIGN

1 point

Nearly all nature areas will have wooden signs with information about the name and distance of the trails. You definitely want to familiarize yourself with the map before you head out, because it can get tricky when you're out there. Everything starts looking alike! You can also look for signs of trailblazing, which has been used for hundreds of years. Trail-blazing is a way people leave clues about which way to go, and it could come in the form of flags, paint, or some other sign.

☐ WATERFALL

3 points

What makes a waterfall? Sometimes
they develop over time because of
erosions in the land. Others have formed
because of natural occurrences like
earthquakes, landslides, glaciers, and
volcanoes. All of these can cause a disruption in the land and/or
watercourse, leading to a waterfall.

☐ HIKING STICK

2 points

Also called trekking poles, hiking
sticks can help you maintain balance,
especially on an uphill, while climbing.
Using sticks in this way can be traced
back to the seventeenth and eighteenth
centuries, when many people also used them as weapons. Today
you can buy hiking sticks in nature shops, or you can just make
your own by finding an old stick that matches your height.

☐ OWL PELLET

3 points

While owl pellets are definitely some
of the best known and easiest to find
animal droppings (look under large
trees), owls aren't the only birds that
produce them. Others include hawks,
herons, gulls, terns, kingfishers, crows, jays, and swallows. Do
a google image search for pellets to see the different sizes and
shapes. This will help you know what to be looking for.

☐ SCAT

2 points

Scat is another word for animal poop, but it's not the only word you can use. Here are a few other words you might see pop up for animal waste: poop, droppings, dung, guano, and manure.

Now you have quite the vocabulary when it comes to describing animals' leavings. See—there's another one!

☐ CHEWED LEAF

1 point

It's not hard to find a leaf with a hole in it or one that has a tear. This is common and part of everyday nature. But it doesn't necessarily mean the leaf has been chewed. To truly find a chewed

leaf, you're probably looking for a small hole that has been made by an insect. Get low to the ground and gently lift up leaves to look for any signs of leaf chewing. You should receive five bonus points on this one if you find an insect in the middle of chewing a leaf!

☐ ANIMAL TRACKS

2 points

Animal tracking is an ancient art that our ancestors used to find and hunt animals. It was probably their best tool available, especially in a time before firearms. Animal tracks are all around

us, but you have to take the time to look. The best time to find fresh tracks is after a light rainfall, when the soil is still soft and makes easy impressions.

☐ MOSS

1 point

Most people think of moss as green fuzzy plants that grow low on trees. While this can definitely be true, this is just one kind of moss. In fact, there are more than 12,000 types of moss all around the world. A lot of mosses can grow up to 4 inches tall; the really big types can get up to 1 foot tall!

☐ WILDFLOWER

1 point

A wildflower is just a flower that is growing in the wild, so a person didn't plant it. There are many different species of wildflowers, which can include natives (plants that are from that area) and nonnatives (plants from other areas). It can be challenging—and fun—to try to identify wildflowers. Get a book from the library or download an app to try to figure out a specific wildflower you find while out hiking.

☐ CHIPMUNK

2 points

Of the twenty-five chipmunk species across the world, twenty-four are found in North America. They can live all over the country in a wide range of habitats. Chipmunks like to hibernate during the cold months, so they gather lots of food like acorns to prepare. A single chipmunk can gather up more than one hundred acorns in a single day.

My Own Hiking Scavenger Hunt Checklist

☐ _____

☐ _____

☐ _____

☐ _____

☐ _____

☐ _____

☐ _____

☐ _____

17 CAMPING SCAVENGER HUNT

Camping is always an adventure, and everyone has favorite things they like to see or do. For some it's going swimming and fishing. For others it's all about the campfire. No matter what you enjoy, there are plenty of scavenger hunt items to look for when camping. Here are a few. Then be sure to create your own list and challenge your family and friends to find your items.

NUMBER OF ITEMS: 8
TOTAL POINTS POSSIBLE: 14

☐ TENT

1 point
Even if you're not using a tent, there shouldn't be one too far away if you're camping. Tents have been around for thousands of years, offering up a quick and easy form of shelter from the weather. Tents got a huge makeover in the 1930s when nylon was invented; now most tents are made from this material.

☐ CAMPFIRE

2 points

You might not think of campfires as being dangerous, but they can be. In just a few short hours, the temperature of your campfire can reach more than 900°F, hot enough to melt metal.

Also, most wildfires originate from campfires that have been abandoned or allowed to get out of control. It's important to always practice good fire safety when you're camping and want to have a fire.

☐ STUMP

2 points

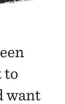

An old stump can be a magical place. It's like a big neon sign for animals. First, it can be a feeding ground. Many insects will use a stump, making it a great place for birds and animals that like to eat bugs. Second, it's a great place for animals to call home. Owls, raccoons, porcupines, and other animals might all want to make a stump their home.

☐ ROASTING STICK

1 point

While you might mostly think of roasting sticks (aka skewers) as being used for roasting marshmallows and meat over a fire, there are a lot more things you can cook on a stick. Test some things out using a little trial and error to see what else you can roast over a fire.

☐ ANIMAL TRACKS

3 points

When you first find an animal track, it's exciting. You might even have some early guesses as to what kind of track you're looking at. But it can be really tricky to distinguish one animal track from another when you're out in the wild. To help identify the track later on, take photos. You'll also want to take measurements if possible. If you don't have anything to measure with, try taking a picture with your hand or even a coin in the photo. This will give you an idea of size when you're looking the track up after your trip. Here's another one where an app or a field guide can help you ID what you're looking at.

☐ FLASHLIGHT

1 point

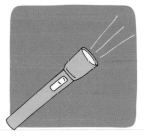

Flashlights first reached the market in 1899, and they make a handy tool to have at night around your campsite. Use them to see where you're going after it's dark and the campfire has died down. You can also shine them around at night if you hear a noise—look for the shiny eyes of a wild animal looking back at you.

☐ FISHING WORMS

2 points

This one is going to take a little extra effort, because you first have to find someone fishing. Then that person has to be fishing with worms. Then you have to see the worm for yourself! The two most popular worms for fishing are red worms, also called earthworms or red wigglers, and nightcrawlers, which do come out at night. If you catch your own worms to take fishing, this will be an easy one to cross off your list.

☐ SLEEPING BAG

2 points

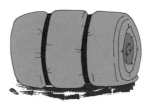

Welshman Pryce Jones created the Euklisia Rug, considered the world's first sleeping bag, in 1876. He even patented his design and accepted mail orders from people who wanted one. He made most of his business by selling them to various armed forces.

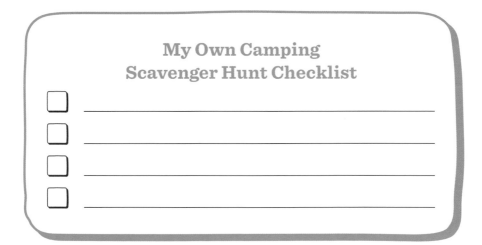

**My Own Camping
Scavenger Hunt Checklist**

☐ _____

☐ _____

☐ _____

☐ _____

18 UNDERWATER SCAVENGER HUNT

With it being underwater, you might think this is going to be a difficult scavenger hunt to conquer. And in some ways, it is. But you can actually knock out many of these items if you know where to look. Even if you don't find all the items right away, keep going back to look. Your patience will eventually pay off, and you can put a check next to every item.

NUMBER OF ITEMS: 10
TOTAL POINTS POSSIBLE: 18

☐ STARFISH

3 points

Most animals have brains and blood, right? That's true, but not starfish. These animals live in the sea—never freshwater—and on average they live about thirty-five years. Look for starfish in tide pools and shallow areas around the ocean.

☐ TADPOLE

3 points

This is how frogs and toads start out—
as tadpoles. When they hatch, they
already have gills like a fish, so they can
breathe under the water. Tadpoles have
really large heads and long tails and are

extremely fast swimmers. You can look along the edge of ponds
and other freshwater sources for tadpoles. You might even
scoop a net down into the water in hopes of finding a tadpole.

☐ FROG

2 points

After tadpoles grow up, they become
frogs (or toads), and there are so many
cool facts about frogs. One is that they
have this really cool skin that absorbs
water. This is how they get water—
absorbing it instead of drinking it.
Another cool fact about frogs is that

they are loud. For many species, you can hear them more than a
mile away!

☐ CLAM OR MUSSEL

1 point

Look down in the water and you should
be able to find a clam or a mussel
pretty easily. If you're at the ocean, you
should get to count oysters on this list

too. Oysters are only found in salt water, but both clams and mussels can be found in salt water or freshwater. They are similar in shape, though. So start peering in that water and see what you can find.

☐ MINNOWS

2 points

Are all small fish minnows? The short answer is no. Minnows are actually a specific fish species that are small in size, which makes them a popular food source for lots of predators. However, for this challenge (since it's hard to tell), you can count any small minnow-like fish.

☐ SEAWEED OR ALGAE

1 point

Are seaweed and algae the same? The answer is yes and no. Seaweed is a type of algae, but they really aren't the same. Algae can be found in both freshwater and salt water, but seaweed is found only in salt water. You can find these plants both on top of the water and down in the water. Start by looking along the edges of waterways to knock this one off your list.

☐ WATER BUG

2 points

This is another one that is a bit tricky. Many people call lots of bugs "water bugs," but there is a true water bug. It's actually supercool, and there are some weird facts you'll want to know. First, it breathes through its butt. Second, it eats lots of mosquito larvae. This is a good thing, so you'll want to thank a water bug next time you see one.

☐ UNIQUE ROCK

1 point

When you're walking along the beach or anywhere near water, you have the potential to find cool rocks. You never know what will wash up on the shore. Plus, rocks that have been in the water tend to have cool layers and textures. They've probably been rolling around in the water for a long time, and all that water and pressure binds material together.

☐ TURTLE

2 points

Are turtles and tortoises the same? No! They are different groups of animals, so don't use the names interchangeably. Turtles mostly live in the water, so they have webbed feet. By comparison, tortoises have very defined toes because they often use them for digging.

☐ SHELL

1 point

You know how important calcium is, right? It makes your bones strong and helps keep you healthy. Well, you have that in common with shells. They are actually made mostly of calcium. This keeps the shells strong as they roll around in the water or along the shore.

My Own Underwater Scavenger Hunt Checklist

☐ _____

☐ _____

☐ _____

☐ _____

☐ _____

☐ _____

☐ _____

☐ _____

19 RARE & UNIQUE SCAVENGER HUNT

This is not going to be an easy scavenger hunt to conquer. Every item on the list is worth three points, and it might take you some time to knock out every single one. But remember this—it will be totally worth it. Some of these items are among the rarest and most unique things you can experience in nature. You won't regret going the extra distance or trying really hard to find each one of them.

NUMBER OF ITEMS: 8
TOTAL POINTS POSSIBLE: 24

☐ DOUBLE RAINBOW

3 points

Whenever you see a double rainbow, it really feels like a magical occurrence. In fact, many cultures consider it a sign of good luck. Double rainbows come from the same set of water droplets that  create the first rainbow. The light is refracted a second time to make a second rainbow. This second one is always lighter than the first one, though. If you see a double rainbow, go ahead and make a wish. Whether it's lucky or not, it doesn't hurt to hope and dream.

☐ ENDANGERED ANIMAL IN THE WILD

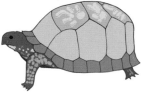

3 points

Endangered animals need our help. Many are losing their habitat, and we need to know about this and spread the word to others. An animal that is endangered in one state might not be in another. To find endangered species by state, visit fws.gov/endangered. Then make it a point to see this animal in the wild and tell others about it.

☐ AURORA BOREALIS

3 points

This is a tough one, and it's all about location. You usually need to be in the far north (like far north in Canada or Alaska) to see the aurora borealis (aka the northern lights). Or you need to be in the far Southern Hemisphere, near the South Pole, where the lights are called the aurora australis. Both occur in high-latitude areas. To find the best places to see these lights, do a web search for tips on where to go and even find a forecast of your chances of seeing the lights in the upcoming days.

☐ FAIRY RING

3 points

Fairy rings are described in old folktales. They've appeared in poems, books, and stories—and in nearly all cases, they are considered a sign of good luck. A fairy ring occurs when mushrooms grow in a circle. As the legend goes, this is because fairies were dancing there. When you find a fairy ring, definitely stand in the center and make a wish.

☐ SUNRISE AND SUNSET IN A SINGLE DAY

3 points

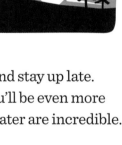

The easiest way to conquer this one is to do it in winter—the days are shorter, so you don't have to wake up so early. If you want to really push yourself, tackle this one in summer, when you have to get up early and stay up late. If you can watch either (or both) over water, you'll be even more impressed. The reflections across and off the water are incredible.

☐ RARE WILDFLOWER

3 points

What's rare in one area won't necessarily be rare in another. To learn about rare plants near you, visit a botanical garden or nature center and talk to the staff. Ask them to tell you about rare flowers in the area and to help you learn to identify them. Don't forget to get a picture for this one!

☐ METEOR SHOWER

3 points

Want to see a meteor shower? These little bits of cosmic debris (what some people call shooting stars) can be more common during certain times of the year—if you know when and where to

look. Usually the best time to watch is very early in the morning on a moonless night. Do a web search of "meteor shower forecast" to find ones coming up near you. Or check with your local astrology group or club.

☐ NESTING ROOKERY

3 points

A rookery is a group of birds all nesting in the same area. This is really cool, because many birds nest alone and are very territorial. In rookeries, however, there are nests everywhere. Some birds that

nest together in a rookery include herons, crows, and spoonbills. If you want to find a rookery, ask a birder you know or visit an online birding site. Many times these birds return to the same spot every year, so birders will be able to tell you where to look.

My Own Rare & Unique Scavenger Hunt Checklist

☐ _____

☐ _____

20 ROCKS & MINERALS SCAVENGER HUNT

If you've never been on a rock hunt, now is the time. It's a different kind of scavenger hunt because it's all about paying attention to small details. Try this hunt in multiple locations—from the beach to the park. It's a fun challenge every time, and no two rocks will ever be the same.

NUMBER OF ITEMS: 8
TOTAL POINTS POSSIBLE: 15

☐ SMOOTH ROCK

1 point

Some of the smoothest rocks you can find are around rivers, oceans, and lakes. As the rocks roll through the water, their surface becomes soft and smooth. Many people use these rocks to make kindness rocks. They paint positive messages or icons on the rocks then set them in public places for others to find and get a fun little surprise.

☐ ROCK WITH FOUR COLORS

2 points

This one isn't going to be that hard, but it's a great challenge to share with family and friends. Have everyone look for the most beautiful rock they can find with as many colors as possible. Set a limit so that everyone has the same search time. When time is up, compare the rocks.

☐ SHINY ROCK

2 points

Have you ever wanted to make your rocks shinier but don't have a rock tumbler? Here's how you do it. First, clean your rocks really well. You can even use an old toothbrush to get in all the crevices. Next, use natural oil like coconut oil or jojoba, which is really more of a wax. This should really give the rocks extra shine for several weeks or months. If they start to fade, just add a little more oil.

☐ BUMPY ROCK

1 point

Have you ever seen a piece of gold? It looks like a bumpy rock in a lot of ways, so keep this in mind when you look for your bumpy rock. Gold is actually a mineral, but it does come from rock.

☐ FUSED ROCK

3 points

A fused rock is another one that you'll want to look for along riverbanks or near other water. This is because the pressure of the water will often fuse rocks together. Eventually, lots of little rock pieces will come together to form one piece. It's cool to find a rock like this while you're out hiking in nature.

☐ FOSSIL IN A ROCK
3 points

There are really rare fossils in rocks
(like dino imprints), and then there are
more common ones. Either way, it's cool
(and pretty challenging) to find a fossil
in a rock. Talk to someone at your local
nature center for help with this one. You might also reach out
to a geology professor at your local college. He or she might be
able to point you in the right direction as well.

☐ PINK ROCK
2 points

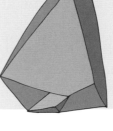

Pink rocks can be found anywhere and
everywhere. Challenge yourself to find a
pink rock at the park, at the beach, and
just out on a hike. You can even start
a pink rock collection . . . or any other
color you like.

☐ ROCK WITH STRIPES
1 point

There are many ways to find rocks
with stripes. Plenty of small rocks have
stripes in parts of them. Another way
to check this one off your list is to look
for a sedimentary rock. This is a type
that forms layers call strata. To see layers of rock like this, look
alongside cliffs or in areas where pieces of rock have broken up.

My Own Rocks & Minerals Scavenger Hunt Checklist

☐ _____

☐ _____

☐ _____

☐ _____

☐ _____

☐ _____

☐ _____

☐ _____

☐ _____

21 TRACKS & SCAT SCAVENGER HUNT

Keep your eyes down during this scavenger hunt. You can learn a lot about what animals are around you when you start looking for and recognizing their different tracks and scat. At first they might all look the same. But if you use a couple of books to become familiar with tracks and scat and learn to recognize them in the wild, you can find out so much on your next hike or walk in the woods.

NUMBER OF ITEMS: 10
TOTAL POINTS POSSIBLE: 20

☐ COYOTE TRACKS

2 points
It can be tricky to tell the difference between a coyote and dog track, but in general, coyote prints usually have the toes closer together than a dog's. Another fun fact about coyotes is that they can walk on their toes. This helps them move quietly so they can sneak up on their prey.

☐ GOOSE SCAT

1 point

Go to any park in the fall, and this one will probably be easy to conquer. It seems like goose poop is everywhere. One reason is that geese poop up to 2 pounds every day. A fun fact about geese is that they often return to the same spot every year to nest. If you always see a goose couple in your area having babies, it could very well be the same pair each year!

☐ SQUIRREL TRACKS

1 point

When squirrels are trying to get away from a predator, they sometimes move in a zigzag pattern, going back and forth as quickly as possible. Keep this in mind when looking for squirrel tracks. It would be fun to find evidence of this pattern!

☐ RABBIT SCAT

1 point

You might have remembered from an earlier fact that bunnies sometimes eat their own poop for extra nutrients—this is true. Another fun fact about rabbits is that in the wild, they don't really eat carrots. Carrots are a root veggie, which rabbits don't eat a lot of. They would rather go for greens, clover, or weeds.

☐ DEER TRACKS

2 points

As a hoofed animal, a deer's tracks can be pretty easy to recognize when you're out in the wild. Remember to look for both small and large tracks, whether you see a fawn (baby deer), a doe (female deer), or a buck (male deer), which is usually the largest. Nearly all deer are born with white spots, but those go away within a year.

☐ MOOSE SCAT

3 points

Moose poop can be very different, based on the time of year you find it. In early summer it's more like a big blob because moose are eating more fresh and juicy leaves, which makes it runny. Later in the season it's in pieces (a lot like pellets) and almost looks like really big rabbit poop. Keep this in mind when you try to check this item off your list.

☐ RACCOON TRACKS

2 points

If you see a print that looks like a tiny baby handprint, you have found a raccoon track. This is because raccoons have five fingerlike toes, which can open wide to handle food. Raccoons are great swimmers and climbers. Mostly they like to be on their own instead of in groups, but the young stay with their mom for about eight to ten months before going out on their own.

☐ BEAVER SCAT

3 points

If you want to see beaver scat, you'd better look around the water, where they make their homes. Beavers usually mate for life and stay together in small groups. It's not uncommon to find a beaver family with young (aka kits) that are multiple ages. They usually stay with their parents for a couple of years before they take off on their own.

☐ TURKEY TRACKS

2 points

Turkeys gobble, right? Well, kinda. It's only the males that gobble, though females will make small noises and pecking sounds. Even though this scavenger hunt item is for turkey tracks, there is a cool fact to know about their poop too. Males make a long, straight poop or a J shape. The poop of female turkeys has a spiral shape.

☐ FOX TRACKS

3 points

This is another one where the track can look a lot like a dog track. A cool fact about foxes is that they have whiskers on both their face and their legs. This helps them navigate, hunt, and figure out where to go next.

My Own Tracks & Scat
Scavenger Hunt Checklist

- [ ] _____
- [ ] _____
- [ ] _____
- [ ] _____
- [ ] _____
- [ ] _____
- [ ] _____
- [ ] _____
- [ ] _____

Chapter 5
DISCOVER NATURE'S PALETTE

What's your favorite color? Do you see it in nature much? This chapter will help you notice just how many amazing and brilliant colors are in the world around us. It's not always going to be an easy scavenger hunt to complete, but it'll definitely keep you looking and paying attention. For all the items in this chapter, be sure to keep an eye out for other colorful items in nature that YOU notice but aren't listed. You'll want to create your own colorful scavenger hunts too. With so many great colors to discover, you had better get started.

22 BLUE SCAVENGER HUNT

The sky is blue. Oceans and lakes are blue. But aside from these obvious ones, what else is on the list? It's not going to be easy to conquer the color blue, but there are a lot of points to rack up. Start looking!

NUMBER OF ITEMS: 10
TOTAL POINTS POSSIBLE: 21

☐ BLUE BIRD

2 points

Yes, you can look for an actual bluebird, but did you know there are several other birds that are blue? There are jays like the blue jay and scrub-jay. There are bright blue birds like the indigo bunting. Then there are birds of a darker blue, like the great blue heron or belted kingfisher. There are others too. Pick up a bird field guide to discover other birds that fall into this blue category.

☐ THE SKY

1 point

Did you know the sky is actually a violet color, but it just looks blue to us? Yep, it's true. It has to do with how the sunlight interacts with the atmosphere and also how our eyes see different kinds of light. Don't worry, it still counts!

☐ PEACOCK

2 points

This bird gets its own entry because it's not native to North America. (All the other birds on this list are.) You'll have to go to a zoo or an animal farm to see a peacock. (Female peacocks, called peahens, don't have bright blue colors like the males, though.)

☐ BLUE FLOWER

3 points

Here's another category that you might not realize has so many options. There are a lot of blue flowers, including blue hydrangea, hyacinth, bluebonnet, balloon flower, delphinium, and morning glory. Blue isn't a common color for flowers, but there are plenty out there to see.

☐ LAKE OR POND

1 point

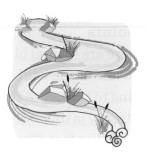

This is another one where you have to ask—is the water really blue? It's actually not—for similar reasons that the sky isn't blue. But it looks blue to the eye, so it definitely counts. Try to find the bluest, clearest water you can for this checklist item.

23 GREEN SCAVENGER HUNT

Green is a sure sign of nature and being outside. It's also a sign of plants, growth, and being healthy. Don't think all the items on the list are going to be growing, though. There are plenty of green things to find that you probably didn't even think of at first.

NUMBER OF ITEMS: 11
TOTAL POINTS POSSIBLE: 18

☐ JAPANESE BEETLE

2 points
Most gardeners will not welcome
Japanese beetles to their yard. These
are annoying insects because they eat
away at healthy plants, causing them to die. These beetles are a bright and shiny green color. If you find one (and they're not that hard to find during growing season), pick them off. Many people put them in a bucket full of soapy water to get rid of them.

☐ PRAYING MANTIS

3 points

Praying mantises have long bodies, long necks, and long legs. In fact, those long front legs are how this insect got its name. When not using them to eat or catch prey, they hold them at an angle, and it looks like they are in a prayer position. The praying mantis is part of the order of mantis insects, and there are more than 2,400 species in the world!

☐ LETTUCE OR SPINACH

1 point

There are so many types of lettuce and spinach to try, so even if you think you don't like it, give it a taste. When you pick lettuce when it's small, it has a really sweet taste too. Plus it's so nutritious. Lettuce is a good source of vitamin C, potassium, calcium, and more!

☐ ALGAE

1 point

Algae is incredibly important, and you probably didn't even know it. Scientists tell us that algae produces more than 70 percent of the Earth's oxygen. Algae also helps remove carbon dioxide from the air. The next time you're outside and take a deep breath, you can thank algae.

☐ CUCUMBER

1 point

If you just ate cucumbers, you'd probably get most of the vitamins you need every single say. It's true. This is a highly nutritious green veggie. A single cucumber gives you vitamins B1, B2, B3, B5, B6, and C, iron, magnesium, folic acid, and more. Cucumbers are mostly water (more than 90 percent), so they'll keep you hydrated too!

☐ MOSS

2 points

Moss doesn't have roots, which is the typical way that most plants absorb water. Instead, water needs to soak into the plant—a lot like a sponge. This is one reason mosses grow so close together in a big clump. It helps the plants hold water as a group for as long as possible.

☐ FISH

2 points

You might think of fish as being pretty plain in color, but they can be really beautiful when you take a closer look. One color that many fish have is green. Some fish have green stripes or even green eyes. If you can find a fish with some green on it *and* green eyes, you should get an extra 2 points for this item.

☐ FROG

1 point

Frogs have these incredible superpowers related to their skin. First of all, they shed their skin as they get bigger and bigger. Then they sometimes eat that skin to give themselves important nutrients. Cool, right? Another cool fact about frogs' skin is that they breathe through it when they're under the water.

☐ HERBS

1 point

Herbs seem to have their own super-powers too. People use many herb plants for medicine and healing. They can be really powerful. One of the top uses for herbs is to cook with them. If you don't cook with fresh herbs, maybe it's time to try. They can add so many flavors when you pick them right off the plant and throw them into whatever you're cooking!

☐ CATERPILLAR

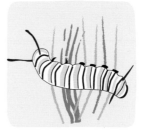

3 points

There are so many cool facts about caterpillars. First of all, they have six legs, just like butterflies. They also have twelve eyes! And they start out really teeny tiny. In fact, as they grow from first hatching out of their egg, their body mass will increase by 1,000 times or more. That's so much! Can you imagine if you got 1,000 times bigger from when you were born?

☐ EVERGREEN

1 point

What is an evergreen? The name is a huge clue—it's a tree that is always green. There are many different types of evergreen trees, and you can find them on every continent except Antarctica. Some of the most famous evergreen trees are the giant sequoias in the redwood forests of California. No matter when you go to see them, they'll be green.

My Own Green Scavenger Hunt Checklist

☐ _____

☐ _____

☐ _____

☐ _____

☐ _____

☐ _____

☐ _____

☐ _____

☐ _____

24 YELLOW SCAVENGER HUNT

This is a color of true happiness. It's hard not to think bright and happy thoughts with the color yellow around. It's also hard not to think of sunflowers. Yes, those are on the list, but there are so many other things aside from flowers to look for. I hope you think positive, cheerful thoughts as you knock off all the items on this hunt.

NUMBER OF ITEMS: 8
TOTAL POINTS POSSIBLE: 15

☐ SUNFLOWER

1 point

It seems like sunflowers have a lot of seeds, especially those big ones, but did you know just how many seeds they have? A single sunflower can have more than 2,000 seeds! If you save a few seeds from your favorite sunflower, you can plant it the next growing season to grow more. Share a few seeds with friends too!

☐ GOLDFINCH

3 points

The American goldfinch is the official bird of three states: New Jersey, Iowa, and Washington. If you think you see a goldfinch outside, listen carefully to see if you can learn its song. One of the calls it makes while flying sounds like *po-ta-to-chip*. This is next level—when you start to recognize birds for their songs, calls, and other noises.

☐ SQUASH

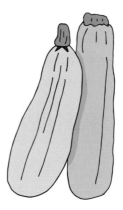

2 points

There are two main types of squash: summer and winter. As you might have guessed, you harvest summer squash earlier and winter squash later on (though it's usually fall, not winter). Squashes are an incredible source of vitamin A. In fact, butternut squash, which can range in color from yellow to orange, provides almost 500 percent of your daily requirement.

☐ ROSE

2 points

Roses come in many colors, and they all mean something different. The yellow rose is a sign of friendship and happiness. If you want to cheer someone up or recognize someone for being a good friend, yellow roses are a great option. Roses come in so many options these days, including thornless! If you like roses, go to your local garden center and ask for a recommendation on what to grow in your area.

☐ SUNRISE

2 points

As the sun rises, its rays are actually white. But because of the beauty of science and the way light refracts in the atmosphere, we get to see gorgeous hues of red, orange, and yellow in the morning.

If you want to see a really good sunrise, arrive before the timetable says the sun actually rises. You won't be disappointed by the extra show as the sun comes up over the horizon.

☐ BABY CHICK

2 points

Baby chicks are some of the cutest and fuzziest baby animals in the world. They are oh so adorable! When chicks are in the egg, they have something call an egg tooth, which helps them peck their way

out of the shell when it's time. After that, they don't really have teeth at all. Instead, they'll peck the ground with their beaks as a way to explore and taste.

☐ BEE

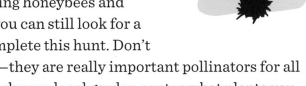

1 point

Believe it or not, not all bees are yellow. But there are plenty of yellow bees out there, including honeybees and bumblebees, so you can still look for a yellow bee to complete this hunt. Don't be afraid of bees—they are really important pollinators for all plants. Instead, ask your local garden center what plants you should grow to support the bee population.

☐ SWALLOWTAIL

2 points

Like most butterflies, swallowtails love warmth. Swallowtails are some of the biggest butterflies you can find in your area, and they have cool caterpillars too. If you want to try attracting them to your garden, consider planting some of their host plans. Host plants are plants that butterflies use to lay their eggs; for swallowtails that includes plants like carrot, fennel, dill, and parsley.

My Own Yellow Scavenger Hunt Checklist

☐ _____

☐ _____

☐ _____

☐ _____

RED SCAVENGER HUNT

Red is one of the boldest colors you can find in nature. From looking up at the sky to looking down on the ground for a really cool (and misunderstood) insect, you will definitely have fun with this list. Red is often an accent instead of being the main color. Keep this in mind the next time you go outside, and see where you can find other signs of red.

NUMBER OF ITEMS: 8
TOTAL POINTS POSSIBLE: 16

☐ SQUIRREL

3 points

The most common squirrel in North America is the gray squirrel, but if you live in an area with red squirrels, you'll definitely notice them. They like to feed on the seeds of conifer cones, so if you don't have a lot of conifers in your area, you might not see one. You might have to travel some to knock this one off your list.

☐ SUNSET

2 points

Many times the sunset is full of rich hues. This has to do with some cool science as the rays of the sun start to lose the blue wavelength hues. You'll see hints of orange and yellow as well, but

red often shows through on really cool nights. This is where the old phrase "Red sky at night, sailor's delight" comes from. (It's a really old saying—ask your parents or grandparents!)

☐ ROSE

1 point

Red roses are definitely signs of love. It's such a classic and beautiful color, and people spend years trying to perfect how to grow beautiful red roses. Roses are a favorite among gardeners. The oldest

known living rose is in Germany, and it's more than 1,000 years old!

☐ ANT

2 points

When it comes to ants, there's a lot of girl power! Most ants stay together in a colony, which is also called a formicary. There is a queen ant, and then all the worker ants are females. So the next

time you see ants walking along and working hard, know that the girls are getting a lot of work done!

☐ MUSHROOMS

2 points

You never know when you'll come across a red mushroom in the wild, but chances are when you do, it'll be in a damp, dark area. This is where you'll usually find mushrooms, and they don't require any sunlight at all to grow! Never ever eat mushrooms from the wild unless you are absolutely sure they're nonpoisonous. You can also look for mushrooms at the local farmers' market. They can add great flavor to dishes and can be really healthy too.

☐ BEE BALM

2 points

Bee balm is a cool plant with an awesome, funky flower on top. It looks kind of like a spider, with little parts of the flower going in every direction. Bee balm can come in many colors, but red is the brightest and most colorful. This plant is very popular with hummingbirds and bees (in case you hadn't guessed that from the name). If you see a hummingbird or bee at this flower, give yourself two more points!

☐ RASPBERRIES

1 point

All over the world, there are more than
200 different types of raspberries.
They don't just come in red either.
Raspberries can be purple, black, even
gold. But for this item, you're looking
for red. You might not always taste it,

but the average raspberry has more than one hundred seeds.
Raspberries are really good for you too—they have more
vitamin C than oranges.

☐ SALMON

3 points

There are several species of salmon,
and they differ in how much red they
have. For instance, the sockeye salmon

is really bright red—it definitely has the most red of all salmon.
For the others, you'll have to look more closely, but many still
have hints of red (or even pink) on them. You might have to
knock this one off your list by making a trip to an aquarium
that has salmon. Otherwise, ask your favorite angler or nature
person for tips on where to find a salmon.

My Own Red Scavenger Hunt Checklist

☐ _____

☐ _____

---

26 BROWN SCAVENGER HUNT

Just as green is a prominent color in nature, so is brown. It really is everywhere, and you might think it's a dull or boring color at first—but it's not. There is so much beauty in this color, but it might take you a little extra looking to appreciate it. Here are some of the great brown sights you can see when you go outside.

NUMBER OF ITEMS: 6
TOTAL POINTS POSSIBLE: 11

☐ WREN

2 points

Wrens are a popular backyard bird throughout North America. They will also use a birdhouse; if you put one out, you just might have a family of wrens make your backyard a home. During springtime, look for wrens and other birds as they gather up nesting material. Grass, feathers, and little twigs are all great for birds. You might see them fly down and then carry material off for their nests. If you get to witness this, give yourself two more points!

☐ ORNAMENTAL GRASS

1 point

Most ornamental grasses are perennials, meaning that once you plant them, they'll come back year after year. Since ornamental grasses are good for butterflies and birds, they are definitely a plant you want to have.

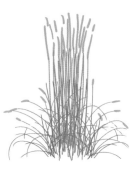

☐ TURKEY

3 points

When you see turkeys, they're often pecking at the ground and moving slow. But they can actually move really fast. They can run up to 25 miles an hour and fly up to 55 miles an hour. And since they are larger birds with a big wingspan, they can actually glide for a long time without flapping their wings. If you happen to look up and see a turkey coasting in the air, this is what it's doing. This would actually be a cool thing to see too. If you do, give yourself another two points.

☐ POTATO

1 point

Like many veggies, potatoes have a lot of water in them—around 80 percent! Potatoes are considered to be very environmentally friendly to grow. This is because they don't require a lot of fertilizer or other material to get them to do well. On average, most Americans eat about 140 pounds of potatoes every single year. The largest potato ever grown weighed more than 18 pounds.

☐ DRIED SEED HEAD

2 points

It's fun to collect seeds from plants, and one of the ways to do this is to go on a seed hunt in late summer or early fall. Look for plants that are past their prime—they probably aren't going to still be blooming. The flowers might be faded or looking dry, and this is what you want. Go up to the flower and see if you can extract the seeds (like with a sunflower). Or give the plant a little shake and see if seeds come out.

☐ HAY

2 points

Do you know how hay is made? Many farmers have hayfields where grass and other plants grow that will make good hay. When it's time to harvest the hay, they cut it with big tractors and then bale it up, usually into rectangular or round bales. This hay will feed their animals in the colder months when there isn't much grass available.

My Own Brown Scavenger Hunt Checklist

☐ _____

☐ _____

☐ _____

☐ _____

☐ _____

☐ _____

☐ _____

☐ _____

☐ _____

27 CAMOUFLAGE SCAVENGER HUNT

Camouflage isn't a color exactly, but you can still have a lot of great camouflage sightings when you're outside. These aren't the camouflage pattern you might be thinking of. Instead, they are animals that have cool camouflage traits, allowing them to blend into their surroundings. This means you'll have to look extra hard for many of them!

NUMBER OF ITEMS: 6
TOTAL POINTS POSSIBLE: 15

☐ KATYDID

3 points

Katydids are most active at night and are loud as they rub their legs together to create a song that sounds like *katy-did, katy-didn't*. During the day they can blend right into trees and branches because they look a lot like a leaf with the way their body gets bigger from front to back. These insects can be between 1 and 5 inches long, and their antennae are two or three times that long.

☐ OWL

3 points

Owls are another nocturnal animal species, so they're most active at night. During the day they'll often find a tree to hang out in to rest and sleep. You might think it's easy to spot them, especially because they can be right out in the open, but it's not. The feather pattern looks a lot like bark, and they can blend right into the tree. If you want to see an owl, try the bird area at a zoo. Or try a nature hike right around dusk. This is one of the best times to see an owl as it starts to come out at night.

☐ RABBIT

1 point

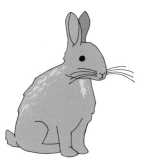

Many rabbits can easily blend into their surroundings, especially if it's the right time of year and the right setting. The arctic rabbit, for example, has a supercool ability to change the color of its fur, from brownish when its environment is more brown and green to white in winter so it blends in with the snow. The gray-brown of other rabbits is perfect for blending into a grassy field.

☐ TURTLE

2 points

Turtles on both land and sea have cool camouflaging powers. Their shells often look like the ground or the bottom of the ocean. This allows them to find a place to settle in without predators finding them. Land turtles often look like rocks when they remain absolutely still. If you go on a nature walk or have the opportunity to see turtles at a zoo or aquarium, try to notice their pattern and how it might easily blend into the wild.

☐ ARCTIC FOX

3 points

Honestly, this one is going to be really tricky to cross off your list, because arctic foxes are mostly located in the far north of North America—Canada and Alaska. Like the rabbit that turns white in winter, it has this same ability. If you can't get this one completed, look for a regular red or gray fox, which is also really good at blending into its surroundings.

☐ WALKING STICK

3 points

Walking sticks are one of the coolest insects you'll ever see, and they might be the best at camouflage on this list. The common walking stick is the one you're most likely to see in North America in the wild. It's a few inches long and looks like a stick. (Yep, the name says it all—it really does look like a stick that is walking.) There are other walking sticks around the world; some can even change color based on their surroundings!

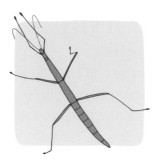

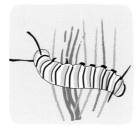

My Own Camouflage
Scavenger Hunt Checklist

☐ _____

☐ _____

☐ _____

☐ _____

☐ _____

☐ _____

☐ _____

☐ _____

☐ _____

Chapter 6
TAKE A TRIP

Who needs a reason to travel? These scavenger hunts will get you going to places near and far. Depending on where you live, you might have a lot of driving (or even flying) to do to get to some of these, but they will definitely be worth it. These scavenger hunts will lead you on some of your greatest outdoor adventures and experiences. There's just something about traveling that makes you notice the world around you more. It's time to start planning your routes!

28 BEACH SCAVENGER HUNT

The beach is one of the all-time awesome destinations for families. It's fun, exciting, relaxing, and so much more. There are plenty of great nature moments and things to see when you're at the beach. Best of all, no two trips are the same. You can do this scavenger hunt over and over again, whether you go back to the same beach or a whole new one. Get ready to fill in your own list too. You'll definitely have some things to add.

NUMBER OF ITEMS: 10
TOTAL POINTS POSSIBLE: 21

☐ DRIFTWOOD

2 points
Driftwood isn't just wood that has washed up on a shore. Well, actually, it is that—but it's also so much more. Driftwood can have a lot of benefits in nature. It can provide homes to animals. It can give birds and insects a place to land when they're out in the middle of the ocean. And it can actually decompose and break down, adding nutrients back into the soil. Driftwood can be beautiful and smooth. Some people use it as art.

☐ SANDCASTLE

1 point

No one quite knows how building sandcastles got started. Some people claim that it dates back to the Egyptians, sculpting little pyramid models out of sand. Regardless, it's a hobby that has been adopted around the world, and it's hard to go to a beach without seeing someone building a sandcastle. It's not just castles that people build, either. All sorts of objects can be made out of sand, and if you're lucky, you'll get to see a sand sculpting competition one day. Better yet, keep practicing, and enter the competition yourself.

☐ KITE

3 points

No one is quite sure who first flew a kite, but this activity has been traced back to ancient China, nearly 3,000 years ago. Kites have a long history of showing up in the military or battles, as certain colors can mean one thing or another. Today kites are used mostly for recreational activities, and you can often find kite shops near beaches because it's naturally windier near open waters. This makes for a great place to go fly a kite!

☐ STARFISH

3 points

Do starfish always have five arms? Nope. There are many different species of starfish (aka sea stars) out there, and while you're most likely to see a starfish with five arms, there are species with seven, ten, twenty, or more arms. By the way, if a starfish loses one of its arms, it can regenerate it. This means the starfish can grow it back.

☐ CRAB

3 points

Both crabs and lobsters are in a group of crustaceans that have ten limbs. When you're on a beach, you're not likely to see crabs just walking on the sand in the middle of nowhere. They are more likely to be crawling through crevices or under rocks. And if you find one crab, chances are there are many more in the area as well, so keep your eyes peeled!

☐ SEABIRD

1 point

This should be an easy one, because almost any bird you see at the beach should count as a seabird, right? Technically this is true, so you should be able to quickly check this one off your list. But here's an extra fact. Many people call all birds along the beach seagulls, but actually there's no such thing as a seagull. Nope, a seagull isn't an official name at all. There are many different types of gulls out there, including the ring-billed and yellow-legged gull, but there's no seagull.

☐ SEA GLASS

2 points

True sea glass takes anywhere from five to fifty years of rolling around in the ocean before it comes out as soft, smooth glass. While most sea glass is just pretty to look at and not valuable, some colors that are rarer than others are sought after. Orange is the rarest color, followed by turquoise and red. Collectors and jewelry makers might pay for sea glass in one of these colors, especially if you find a really big piece.

☐ TIDE POOL

3 points

Do you know how tide pools are formed? Well, you know the ocean is constantly in motion, so the tide will come in and go out every single day. As certain areas erode away, it creates little holes or crevices in the shore. When it's high tide, these crevices are completely covered with water. But at low tide the water stays in these holes to create little pools where sea creatures often hang out. During low tide, you can walk out to peer inside! If you go to explore tide pools, be sure to wear sturdy sneakers or water shoes—and don't get caught up in the tide coming back in. You usually have only a short time for exploring.

☐ SAILBOAT

2 points

Sailboats aren't exactly fast—most only go between 4 and 7 miles per hour (or 4 to 6 knots, as most sailors would say). But if you were on a longer boat, you'd be able to go faster. One of the reasons people like to go sailing is that they're able to get to places that other people can't access by land or a bigger boat. If you're interested in sailing, you should check out a local sailing club near you. Many places will give free sailing lessons to kids or provide the opportunity to go out on a sailboat.

☐ BEACH BUG

1 point

This is another one that should be pretty easy to check off your list, because any bug on the beach will count. Here's a challenge, though. Try to capture a photo of a bug or insect on the beach and then figure out what it is. You can try to look it up online or ask other beachgoers. This truly takes your curiosity about nature to another level.

My Own Beach Scavenger Hunt Checklist

- [ ] _____
- [ ] _____
- [ ] _____
- [ ] _____
- [ ] _____
- [ ] _____
- [ ] _____
- [ ] _____
- [ ] _____
- [ ] _____

29 NATURE CENTER SCAVENGER HUNT

Nature centers are true gems of the community. They usually have really knowledgeable and passionate staff that know a lot about the area and all the nature in it. If you have hiking trails near you with a nature center, be sure to check the hours, and make a point to go when it's open. Sure, you could just enjoy the trails outside of hours, but it's great to take the time to actually go into the building and see what else you can learn. (*Psst!* You'll definitely learn something new!)

NUMBER OF ITEMS: 8
TOTAL POINTS POSSIBLE: 14

☐ BIRD FEEDER

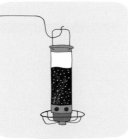

1 point
There are so many different types of bird feeders out there. You have a suet feeder, which is often square and usually holds suet to attract birds like woodpeckers. Then there are tray and hopper feeders that hold most types of birdseed and can attract a large number of different birds. A bird feeder with a fancy setup will have a squirrel baffle as well. This is usually a cone shape about three-fourths of the way up the pole to help prevent squirrels from crawling up the pole and stealing all the seed.

☐ WILDFLOWERS

2 points

Wildflowers vary a lot by region, and what's native in one area will be different for another. For this challenge, try to see (and identify) three different wildflowers. The seeing part will be easy, but then it's important to ID them. For this, ask the staff at the nature center, showing them pictures you've taken. Or use a book focusing on wildflowers in that area. Google can help a ton, too, if you're able to describe the flower (example: Wildflower in July in Wisconsin that is red).

☐ CHIPMUNK

2 points

Did you know that most chipmunks live underground? Yep. They are a lot like mice, burrowing in and creating a home under your feet. They can have a tunnel that is 20 feet or more. They often live together too—in this case, a group of chipmunks is called a scurry.

☐ SQUIRREL

1 point

The tail of a squirrel is both fascinating and functional. First, it's a communication tool. For instance, if a squirrel flicks its tail three times in a row, it might be warning other nearby squirrels of danger. The squirrel's tail is also a good tool for staying warm or cool. On cold nights, squirrels can wrap their tail over their body to stay cozy. In summer, they have this cool ability to pump more blood to their tail, lowering their body temperature.

☐ TURTLE

2 points

Turtles eat a lot of different types of food, depending on where they live. For instance, a sea turtle might eat algae or animals like squid and jellyfish. On land, turtles will eat berries, grass, and beetles. Many nature centers will have pet turtles. Ask when feeding time is, because this is a cool thing to watch in person.

☐ AMAZING NATURE FACT

3 points

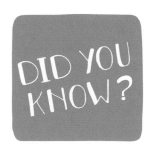

Nature centers should be filled with amazing facts, and they are—as long as you know where to look. First off, remember the staff of the nature center, and be open to learning from them. They often have lots of cool things to share, so check out a nature program (often free) where you can learn for yourself. Another way to find cool facts is to just read. Many nature centers will have information displayed. You just have to take the time to look for it.

POND

2 points

This is one that either exists or doesn't at the nature center you're visiting. You can't really "find" a pond that isn't there, even if you look really hard. If you happen to be going to a nature center with a pond, challenge yourself to see and track as many different animals as you can while on a single walk. Another fun challenge is to set a timer to see how many animals you can find in 10 or 15 minutes. If you aren't going to a nature center with a pond, save this checklist item to mark off another time.

☐ DEAD TREE

1 point

As long as a dead tree does not have a disease or something else wrong with it, nature centers like to leave some up because they are such good resources for animals. They offer homes to small mammals like raccoons, as well as

insects and birds. Challenge yourself to find a dead tree and also a hole where an animal could be living.

My Own Nature Center Scavenger Hunt Checklist

- [ ] _____
- [ ] _____
- [ ] _____
- [ ] _____
- [ ] _____
- [ ] _____
- [ ] _____
- [ ] _____
- [ ] _____

30 PUBLIC GARDEN SCAVENGER HUNT

Public gardens can be small and unofficial, like great gardens at a library, a city hall, or just a public park. Or they can also be more formal, like a botanical garden with set hours and an entry fee. Try looking for both in your community and especially when you travel. Public gardens want the public to come and visit, so if you happen to be on vacation or passing through a town, do a quick little search to see if there's a public garden nearby. It's a good way to take a break and enjoy some beautiful flowers at the same time.

NUMBER OF ITEMS: 8
TOTAL POINTS POSSIBLE: 16

☐ RED FLOWER

1 point

Any red flower will do, but here's a fact about the flower pictured here—a red zinnia. Zinnias are easy flowers to grow from seed. So get yourself a seed packet in the spring and grow a whole patch

from seed to flower. Also, they are quite popular with bees and butterflies because they are a good source of nectar. Zinnias tend to grow up to a foot tall and can have blooms that are ball shape or more like a daisy.

☐ PINK FLOWER

1 point

The pink flower pictured here is a purple coneflower. Yes, even though purple is in its name, it's usually pink. At least the native ones are. Nowadays you can find coneflowers that are yellow, orange, red, and green. The purple coneflower is fairly easy to grow, and it will come back year after year on its own. Plus it multiplies. So when you buy one coneflower plant, it might multiply to three or four plants in just a few short years.

☐ BLUE FLOWER

3 points

The color blue is not common in flowers, so you have to take anything you get. Even a deep purple might have to count as blue if you're having trouble checking this one off your list. One of the easiest ways to see a blue flower is by finding blue hydrangeas, pictured here. This is a type of shrub, and the flowers are big and beautiful. Hydrangeas are also common as pink or white flowers.

☐ YELLOW FLOWER

1 point

The black-eyed Susan is a common yellow flower that you've probably seen before—even if you didn't know the name. This is another one that is easy to grow. It comes back year after year, and it will even tolerate really dry conditions. The botanical name (aka scientific name) for this flower is rudbeckia, and many people call it this instead.

☐ SHRUB WITH FLOWER

3 points

This item gets a higher point value because it's not always easy to find a shrub with a flower. Usually the flowers are short-lived because they go on to become fruit. The best time of year to see shrubs with flowers is spring. The shrub pictured here is forsythia. With its sunny yellow flowers, it is one of the brightest and most colorful shrubs. However, those blooms only last a couple of weeks, which is why any shrub with a flower gets you more points.

☐ SHRUB WITH THORNY BRANCHES

2 points

There are a lot more shrubs with thorny branches than you might think. This item will have you getting really close to plants so you can get a good look. For instance, roses would count on this list. (As long as it's not a thornless rose you're looking at.) Another thorny shrub you'll find at most public gardens is hawthorn. Now don't go poking the shrub to find out if it's thorny—that'll hurt. You should be able to see just fine with your eyes alone.

☐ TREE WITH MARBLED TRUNK

3 points

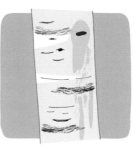

The paper birch, pictured here, is definitely a tree that will count for this list item. Paper birches have the coolest bark, which looks like paper. (Don't peel it off, though.) Any tree (or shrub, if you have a hard time finding a tree) should count for this item. It's another one that will require you to look up close. You might be surprised to see just how cool and pretty the bark of a tree can be.

☐ FLOWER TALLER THAN 6 FEET

2 points

This should be an easy one to knock off your list, depending on the time of year. If you're going in spring, the flowers  might not be that tall yet. However, if you go in summer, this should be no problem. The flower pictured here is a sunflower, and it can easily grow to be 6 to 8 feet tall. Other tall flowers include cannas, joe-pye weed, and hollyhocks.

My Own Public Garden Scavenger Hunt Checklist

☐ _____

☐ _____

☐ _____

☐ _____

☐ _____

☐ _____

☐ _____

☐ _____

☐ _____

31 STATE PARK SCAVENGER HUNT

Our public parks are so important to each state. This is land that has been set aside by the state to protect and make available for all to use. It takes a lot of work to maintain these lands. You can help, though! By just visiting your state park and paying the small fee, you're giving some much-needed support. Another big thing you can do while at a park is to clean up after yourself and never throw garbage where it doesn't belong. This is one of the biggest expenses for public parks, and it's such a small thing you can do to help! Here are some items to look for when you next visit at a state park.

NUMBER OF ITEMS: 8
TOTAL POINTS POSSIBLE: 13

☐ ACORN

2 points
Acorns come from oak trees, so you need to be at a place that has oak trees to check this one off your list. If you're not sure how to recognize an oak tree, look up oak leaves. They have a couple really distinct shapes, depending on the species, so this will definitely help you. If you still have trouble finding oak trees in your area, ask around or talk to the staff at state park offices for their tips on where to look.

☐ AMPHIBIAN

3 points

To be able to check this one off the list, you have to know what to look for. How well do you know your amphibians? The most likely contenders include a frog, a toad, or a salamander. Remember that amphibians like to stay cool and damp, so look near water or swampy areas. If you find more than one type of amphibian, give yourself an extra point.

☐ POISON IVY

2 points

Have you heard the little rhyme "Leaves of three, let it be"? This is a really easy way to remember what to look for when it comes to poison ivy. Of course not every green plant with three leaves is going to be poison ivy, but until you learn to recognize it, the rhyme is a good place to start. Poison ivy can be low to the ground or grow more like vines, upward. Keep an eye out for both.

☐ MUSHROOM

2 points

People who eat mushrooms really do love them. They are in so many dishes and are often nicknamed "the meat of the vegetable world." Not all mushrooms should be eaten—some can be deadly poisonous. To find a mushroom for this hunt, be sure to look in shady, damp areas, where they most like to grow.

☐ TREE STUMP

1 point

If you're at a state park, there are two
likely places you'll see a tree stump.
First, you might just see one out in the
woods after trees have been cut down. There might also be a
stump if a tree has fallen down. The other spot would be in a
community area or around a fire pit where they are using tree
stumps as seats. Either way, this one shouldn't be too hard to
check off.

☐ TINY BUG

1 point

Here's another one that can be a fun
mini challenge in and of itself. Since
"tiny bug" is pretty vague and could
include lots of different bugs, make
this item a friendly little competition.
(You can work in partners or by yourself.) Set the timer for
15 minutes and try to find the teeniest, tiniest bug you can. If
you're all in the same area, share your sighting with others.
If you're far apart, take a picture of your bug so everyone can
compare at the end.

☐ FALLEN LOG

1 point

All parks—local, state, or national—
should have fallen logs. It's just what
happens—logs fall in the forests. As an added challenge, try to
walk along the fallen log. Definitely do this at your own risk.

Some logs can be too small or unstable to do this safely. Plus, you don't want to go off-trail too much to accomplish this one. But if you have a really sturdy fallen log, try to walk along it and capture a picture while doing so.

☐ PICNIC TABLE

1 point

No one knows the definite history of picnic tables, but many people say they've been around since the late 1800s.

Picnic tables are popular in public places because you can fit so many more people on the benches than traditional chairs. For an extra point on this item, be sure to take a picnic lunch and eat it at the picnic table.

**My Own State Park
Scavenger Hunt Checklist**

☐ _____

☐ _____

☐ _____

☐ _____

☐ _____

☐ _____

☐ _____

☐ _____

32 NATIONAL PARK SCAVENGER HUNT

Like state parks, national parks are important public lands that have been set aside and designated for all to use. In many cases they protect national treasures, endangered animals, and habitat that we wouldn't otherwise have. With more than sixty national parks to choose from, visiting one is usually an entire vacation for many people. Save this scavenger hunt to do again and again with each national park you visit. You'll definitely find it's easier (or harder) to complete, based on where you go.

NUMBER OF ITEMS: 8
TOTAL POINTS POSSIBLE: 13

☐ ANIMAL HOME
2 points

This one is wide open for you to interpret. Should it be an animal home up in the trees, like a nest? Should it be a home down in the ground, like a fox burrow? Maybe you even want to find an animal home in a tree. If you find this one really easy to do, challenge yourself to find multiple types of animal homes.

☐ REPTILE

3 points

Do you know what makes a reptile different from an amphibian? Two big ones are that reptiles are covered in scales and also have claws on their toes—neither of which an amphibian can claim. Some of the reptiles you're most likely to see at a national park include lizards, snakes, and turtles. If you're in the right area, you might also see an alligator, though some people might not want to spot one of those.

☐ MAMMAL

1 point

This one is another easy category, so it's time to play a game. Any mammal can count—big or small—so now your job is to see how many different types of mammals you can spot during your trip to a national park. You can either make this a daily challenge or count them up for your entire trip if you're going for multiple days. You should stop at the visitor center to ask for tips on where to spot cool mammals in the park.

☐ THORNY PLANT

2 points

First of all, stay away from thorny plants. They can stick or poke you, causing pain or irritation for several days. However, this is a fun one on the list because it really makes you pay close attention to details. Get up close to trees, shrubs, and plants. Look for those thorns, and then mark it complete.

☐ DEAD TREE

1 point

This item is on the nature center scavenger hunt list, and it belongs on this one too. Management at every good park likes to leave nature as they find it as much as possible. This means that when a tree dies, it's allowed to break down and decompose naturally. This is good for animals and the habitat in the area. Plus, it's a cool opportunity to see an owl (or another animal) making the dead tree its home.

☐ LAKE OR POND

1 point

Here's a tip: If there's a lake or a pond at a national park, it's going to be a very popular spot. This is because it's probably one of the best opportunities to see wildlife in their natural environment. Plan to visit the pond or lake early in the day, before it gets really busy with other visitors. Most parks will have a hiking trail around a lake or pond, and it'll be a great experience.

☐ PARK RANGER

2 points

You might see a park ranger out on the trails at a national park. But your best chance to see and talk to a ranger is going to be at the visitor center. Almost all national parks have a visitor center, and they keep it staffed with at least one park ranger, who is there to answer your questions. They'll give you tips about what's going on in the park and what activities might be a good fit for your family. When you see park rangers, thank them for their service. They are in a public job, serving you, and they would definitely appreciate a word of thanks.

☐ TRAILHEAD

1 point

Sometimes trailheads are really clearly marked; other times they aren't at all. It depends on the park and the popularity of the trail. If you're looking for a specific trail, save yourself some time and go into the visitor center. The helpful staff will give you advice on a good trail for you to take—they know the difficulty levels. Plus, they'll give you maps and tell you what to look for so you can find that trailhead sign and know you're headed in the right direction.

My Own National Park Scavenger Hunt Checklist

☐ _____

☐ _____

☐ _____

☐ _____

☐ _____

☐ _____

☐ _____

☐ _____

33 WILDLIFE REFUGE SCAVENGER HUNT

Wildlife refuges are similar to state or national parks because they are public lands, set aside by our government. But in this case, they have been set aside to protect wildlife in the area. Often these areas have unique habitat that needs to be preserved in order to protect and support certain animals. Refuge visitor centers often have specific hours, so try to visit when they are open. You'll learn a lot from the staff and inside displays.

NUMBER OF ITEMS: 8
TOTAL POINTS POSSIBLE: 15

☐ ANIMAL TRACKS

2 points

Did you know that animal tracks can actually become fossils? They can! In fact, you could even come across an animal track imprint in sandstone or another rock. You can also create your own sort of fossil by making a cast out of plaster. You fill an animal track you find in the wild with plaster. After you give the cast time to dry, you should be able to pull it out of the ground, and then you have the track imprint!

☐ TREE WITH WOODPECKER HOLES

1 point

Do you know why woodpeckers peck holes? There are a couple of reasons: They might be looking for sap or for insects. These holes start off small, but they can keep going and going, getting bigger as a place for animals to hide food and nuts. Or they might get really big and become a place where birds or animals build a nest.

☐ TREE WITH ANTLER RUBBINGS

3 points

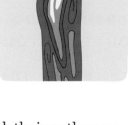

Deer rub their antlers on trees for several reasons. Bucks might do this in fall because they are rubbing off the velvety texture that has grown on their antlers over the summer. They might also rub their antlers on trees in the spring as a way to mark their territory, warning other male deer to go away. Trees with antler rubbings look very bare, and for young trees, it can actually cause a lot of damage.

☐ HAWK SOARING

2 points

Hawks are the top of the food chain, just like owls and eagles, so they don't have a lot of predators after them. You might see hawks hanging out in trees or on telephone poles, waiting to swoop down on prey like rabbits, smaller birds, and foxes. Even though hawks hunt smaller birds, sometimes these smaller birds will gang up on the hawk and chase and peck it. This usually occurs during nesting season, and it tells the hawk to get out of their territory.

☐ SOMEONE WITH BINOCULARS
2 points

Because wildlife refuges have been set aside to help protect natural areas and important habitat, they are a great place to see birds. If you're out and about and see someone with binoculars, be friendly and ask what he or she is seeing or looking for. Birders often like to share information and bird sightings with others. Some even carry a spotting scope—and are happy to let you look through it so you can see the bird too.

☐ NEST IN A TREE
1 point

Sometimes we forget to look up because we're so focused on what is in front of us. So for this scavenger hunt item, challenge your family and friends to go on a nest hunt with you. Set a timer for 15 or 20 minutes, and then go in teams or groups. See how many nests you can spot during this time. Look for nests big and small. It's easy to find the bigger ones, like squirrel nests; it's even more fun and challenging to look for smaller ones.

☐ BRIDGE

1 point

A bridge can be really big and bold—or it can be really small and simple. The earliest bridges were likely just fallen logs or stepping-stones to get people from one area to another. As bridges advanced, many had the arch shape that we think of today. As you look for your bridge for this list, keep in mind that the simple ones should count too. You might even find an animal-built bridge in a lake or pond.

☐ 3 WILD ANIMALS

3 points

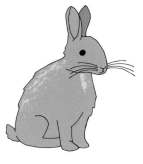

Since a refuge has "wildlife" in its name, it's definitely a good idea to look for some wildlife while you are here. This one shouldn't take you too long to do, but make sure you find three different types. You can't count three different birds for this one. Try doing a little prediction before you go to the wildlife refuge about what you might see, and then discover which animals you actually do. It's a fun challenge and a good way to get your family talking.

My Own Wildlife Refuge
Scavenger Hunt Checklist

☐ _____

☐ _____

☐ _____

☐ _____

☐ _____

☐ _____

☐ _____

☐ _____

☐ _____

MOUNTAINS SCAVENGER HUNT

What are the closest mountains to you? Depending on where you live, this might be a very easy scavenger hunt to complete, or it might be one you have to tackle while on vacation. There are many great mountains to visit in North America, but it's definitely a more challenging scavenger hunt to complete. You might not get everything in one visit, but don't give up. Keep going to the mountains until you can cross every item off your list.

NUMBER OF ITEMS: 8
TOTAL POINTS POSSIBLE: 18

☐ ELEVATION SIGN

1 point

If you're in the mountains, there's a good chance you're going to see an elevation sign. However, you might have to do some hiking or climbing to get to it. Often on mountain hikes, the trail will have elevation markers to help you know how much farther you need to go. Once

you reach the top, be sure to take a picture. This is proof that you were there and made the climb (or drive, in some cases).

☐ SNOW

3 points

Not all mountains have snow, but many do. Even in summer, you should be able to see hints of snow when you're in and around the mountains. But why is there more snow on top of a mountain? It has

to do with altitude. As you get higher and higher on a mountain, the air pressure decreases. At the same time, warm air rises and the moisture in that air expands and cools, turning into rain and often snow when it's cold enough.

☐ MOUNTAIN ANIMAL

3 points

It can be challenging to see an animal when you're hiking or exploring a mountain. You might have hopes of seeing a bear, moose, elk, or other big mammal, but they aren't usually just

out in the open. You'll have to really be on the lookout—and get lucky too! Any animal should count for this challenge, but take a bonus point if you see one of the big ones mentioned here.

☐ BENCH

1 point

When you go on a hike, especially one
that is challenging or has a lot of high
elevation, one of the most welcome
sights you can come across is a bench.
If you find a bench but haven't yet done
your hike, then use it as your post-hike reward. Go out and
really conquer that walk or hike, then take a well-deserved rest!

☐ LOOKOUT AREA

2 points

As you drive up a mountain, it's not
safe to stop—even if you see the most
gorgeous view. This is why there are
lookout or pullout areas along the drive.
These are designated safe places to
stop, get out, and snap a picture. Some lookouts also have signs
with cool facts. If you happen to be at a bigger lookout area, see
what you can learn. You might even want to stop off at all the
lookouts—you'll get new pictures and learn different facts at
each one.

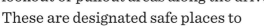

☐ WATERFALL

3 points

If there's a visitor center in the area, stop and ask the staff if there are any waterfalls to see. They're going to know where they are, how to get there, and if they water is flowing right now. It's well worth the stop to get this information. If there's no visitor center or it's closed, definitely keep an eye out when you're in the mountains. Often you'll come across a tiny waterfall that has just been created because of natural elements like melting snow or extra rain. These are so much fun to find, and they definitely count.

☐ AMAZING VIEW

2 points

This one is really open to interpretation. What's an amazing view to one person might just be so-so to another. But this is for you to decide. And don't stop at just one amazing view. If you're in the mountains, try to collect as many amazing views as you can. You'll especially want to get a photo at sunset, when the sun seems to drop down over the mountains right before your eyes.

☐ MOUNTAIN BIRD

3 points

There are some really great mountain birds, and often they are unique to mountainous areas. This is another good one where you might want to stop at the local visitor center and ask the staff what birds to look for. Mountain bluebirds and mountain chickadees are a couple birds you might want to look for. The visitor center staff will likely have many more to suggest.

My Own Mountains
Scavenger Hunt Checklist

- [ ] _____
- [ ] _____
- [ ] _____
- [ ] _____
- [ ] _____
- [ ] _____
- [ ] _____
- [ ] _____
- [ ] _____

Chapter 7
SEASONS

Do you have a favorite season? This chapter of scavenger hunts it all about the four seasons. The items listed are some of the most typical things you might see during a certain time of year . . . plus a few surprises thrown in along the way. You might find some of the items really easily; others might take you weeks to spot. If you finish off a list early in the season, challenge yourself to tackle it again later on. Then compare the results from one time to the next. No matter what, these challenges make a great reason to get outside, no matter the season.

35 SPRING SCAVENGER HUNT

After the long, dark days of winter, spring is such a welcoming season. It's a time of new life and growth everywhere you look. This scavenger hunt has some of the most iconic symbols of spring across the country. You might not see everything in a single day, but try to find everything on the list during the official days of spring. Then be sure to add your own spring list at the end. The season is slightly different for all, based on where you live. It'll be fun to document what happens in your area in spring so you can look for those items again next year.

NUMBER OF ITEMS: 10
TOTAL POINTS POSSIBLE: 16

☐ BABY BUNNY
2 points

This is an item you'll want to check off the list early in the season; otherwise, baby bunnies grow too quickly and look just like adults. But when they are still young, you can definitely see a difference in size. Babies have a lot more fluff as well as ears that are shorter overall. They stick around their parents at first too. So if you see an adult bunny and it's early spring, keep an eye out for any babies that might be nearby.

☐ BIRD'S NEST

2 points

Yes, birds' nests are in trees and birdhouses, but there are other places to look for nests too. For instance, American robins build their nests in trees but also on window ledges, in hanging baskets of plants, and even on porch lights. They just look for a place that is tucked away from the weather, and then it's fair game. So when hunting for a nest to cross off your list, don't just look in trees. They can definitely be found in other places.

☐ TULIP

1 point

If it seems like tulips come and go quickly, you're right. They only bloom for three to seven days before they fade away, so they really do have a short life. A cool fact about tulips is that there are so many different types. There are more than 150 different species, 3,000 varieties, and they come in almost every color. Remember, if you want to have tulips in your backyard, be sure to plant them in fall.

☐ DAFFODIL

1 point

Daffodils are one of the earliest flowers that bloom in spring. They will even start growing through the snow, peeking through on warmer days. Daffodils are popular throughout the world and are symbolic to many. For some they are signs of happiness and good fortune. For others they represent hope. They are also the official flower of March. If you want to give a friend or loved one flowers in March, daffodils are definitely a good choice.

☐ BLOOMING TREE OR SHRUB

1 point

Spring is the peak time for blooming trees and shrubs. The blooms don't usually last long, but they are gorgeous in the moment. This shouldn't be a difficult item to check off your list, so make it a little more challenging by finding a new blooming tree or shrub every few days. One of the earliest bloomers is the redbud tree, which starts its deep, rich pink color in late winter or very early spring. Forsythia is another fun one to look for, because this is a shrub with bright yellow blooms. How many different blooming trees and shrubs can you find (and identify) this season?

☐ RAINBOW

3 points

You've probably heard of or even seen a rainbow, but have you ever heard of a fogbow or a moonbow? Fogbows occur out of fog where clouds and water droplets align to create faint colors. A 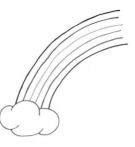 moonbow is a rarity, but it occurs at night when the light from the moon shines and hits water droplets in a certain way. If you see either of these unique types of rainbows, give yourself two extra points.

☐ PUDDLE

1 point

Puddles can be a great place for bugs, butterflies, and bees to stop for a drink. Adding water is one of the most important things you can do to attract  life to your backyard. So think about creating your own little puddle by digging out a hole and keeping it filled with fresh water. The butterflies and other insects will really appreciate it.

☐ DANDELION

1 point

Dandelions start out as yellow flowers but turn into those white puffs filled with seeds. As the tradition goes, you can pick a dandelion puff, make a wish, and then try to blow all the seeds away  at once for a chance to have your wish to come true. Once dandelion seeds hit the wind, they might travel for miles before they land to grow a new plant the next year.

☐ SPROUT

1 point

Have you ever heard of microgreens? These are actually just little sprouts from plants like sunflowers, lettuce, and more. Chefs love microgreens because  they have so many nutrients and flavors. They will plant hundreds of seeds at a time in order to have lots of microgreens for their dishes. You can try this too. Grow little sprouts from a packet of seeds, and then gently pick them off when they are only a couple inches tall. Give these sprouts a taste and see if you like the flavor.

☐ FEATHER

3 points

As seasons change, birds go through something called molting, where they lose feathers and grow new ones at the same time. If you find a feather on the ground, it might be because a bird was molting. Just leave it on the ground, though. Birds often take these feathers and use them to build their nests. They are good for making soft, cushy nests for the baby birds.

My Own Spring Scavenger Hunt Checklist

☐ _____

☐ _____

☐ _____

☐ _____

☐ _____

☐ _____

☐ _____

☐ _____

☐ _____

36 SUMMER SCAVENGER HUNT

If you ask people what their favorite season is, there's a good chance that most will say summer. Whether that's because most schools are off or because of the great weather, it really is a great season with a lot of activity and nature life. Here are some of the most commons things you should look for this summer. Really try to take the time to experience them all.

NUMBER OF ITEMS: 8
TOTAL POINTS POSSIBLE: 16

☐ CLOVER

2 points

It's common to see a patch of clover in summer, growing in sunny backyards, and most of those plants will have three leaves. But have you ever found a four-leaf clover? They are definitely a lot rarer; you'll only find one four-leaf clover for every 10,000 three-leaf clovers. If you do find one, go ahead and make a wish. For hundreds of years, people have thought of four-leaf clovers as lucky, so you don't want to miss your chance to make a wish.

☐ WATERMELON

1 point

Did you know that watermelons are considered both a fruit and a vegetable? They are! Plus, they are the official state vegetable of Oklahoma. This popular summer treat is more than 90 percent water, so it's no wonder that "water" is in the name. Watermelons naturally have seeds in them, but some have been developed by growers over the years to be seedless. (They might still have some clear or pale seeds, but those are edible.) While most people eat the inside of watermelons, you can actually eat the rinds too.

☐ BUMBLEBEE

2 points

There are more than 250 bumblebee species, and they spend a lot of their days visiting flowers and collecting pollen, just like other bees. Unlike bees that live in big colonies, bumblebees tend to stay in smaller groups. But where do they go in winter? They actually hibernate under the ground until it's warm again.

☐ ANT
1 point

Ants don't have ears like most animals. This doesn't mean they can't hear, though. They just do it in a different way. Ants feel vibrations through the ground, and they have special sensors on their feet and in their knees that help them know what's going on around them. They have tiny little hairs all over their body to help in sensing what's around them too.

☐ GRASSHOPPER
3 points

How do grasshoppers jump so high? Their hind legs are actually like little catapults. When grasshoppers are ready to jump, they sit back on their hind legs, almost like a springboard, and then shoot up through the air. Most grasshoppers can jump up to 3 feet high. Then, with the help of their wings, they can quickly move big distances.

☐ SUNFLOWER OVER 6 FEET
3 points

There are two main types of sunflower seeds. One type of seed is black, which is often used to make sunflower oil or margarine for cooking. The other type of seed is striped, which is what you'll buy to eat or use as birdseed. The next time you see a sunflower, get up close to it to see what type of seeds it has.

☐ SUMMER BERRIES

1 point

Much like fall is the season for apples, summer is the season for berries. From strawberries (which can be a spring fruit, but some varieties produce all summer) to summer blueberries and raspberries, there are so many berry options to enjoy during the summer. See how many different types of summer berries you can find and taste.

☐ BUTTERFLIES (5 DIFFERENT TYPES)

3 points

Summer is the peak time for butterflies because they thrive in hot, sunny weather. Butterflies like monarchs and swallowtails are easy to spot because they are so big. But others, like skippers and painted ladies, aren't as easy to recognize. This summer, see how many different types of butterflies you can see. Don't just stop at five; keep going. How many can you see before the end of summer?

My Own Summer Scavenger Hunt Checklist

☐ _____

☐ _____

☐ _____

☐ _____

37 FALL SCAVENGER HUNT

If fall is your favorite season, you probably like cooler weather that requires only a sweatshirt or light jacket. Signs of fall include leaves changing color, pumpkins, apples, and preparing for winter, and the items on this list definitely reflect all of those and more. Fall is a great time of year to get out and be active. It's usually not too hot or cool but just right as you go out to enjoy nature. Here are some of the most common fall items you can check off one at a time.

NUMBER OF ITEMS: 8
TOTAL POINTS POSSIBLE: 16

☐ PINECONE

1 point
Did you know there are male and female pinecones? Yep, the big cones that most people think of as pinecones are the females. The male pinecones are much smaller and often go unnoticed. Another fun fact about pinecones is that they can stay on the tree for ten years or more before they drop down! Some people think they drop every year, but that's not always the case.

☐ LADYBUG

2 points

Many ladybugs can live for two or three
years. This is pretty good, considering
that butterflies might only live for a
couple of weeks and many bees die off
each year. When it's fall, ladybugs will look for a place to stay
and hibernate during the cold months. Then on warm days,
they come out, ready to explore. One more fun fact about
ladybugs is that when they beat their wings, they go at a rate of
around 5,100 times a minute!

☐ LEAVES (5 DIFFERENT COLORS)

3 points

You should go on a leaf hunt at least
once every fall. The best time to go is
when the colors are at their peak and
falling quickly. Try to find at least five
different leaves and colors. Look for the brightest, prettiest
leaves on the ground, and then try to identify the tree they came
from. You can use a field guide for this, look online, or try an
app. Don't forget to take a picture!

☐ ACORN

2 points

Animals love acorns, but can you eat them? Yes, you can, but they will probably taste bitter to you. They also have natural tannins that might not make your tummy feel great. If you want to try some acorns for yourself, you might want to soak them in water (or even boil them) first. Some people use acorns to make something called acorn coffee.

☐ APPLES (3 DIFFERENT TYPES)

3 points

Fall is a great time to go apple picking. Search online to find spots for apple picking in your area. When you go, try to branch out and try a few different varieties—not just the ones you eat all the time. Another tip is to go apple picking at different times of the season. The varieties available are very much about timing, and they go quick! If you show up at an apple place two weeks apart, there will likely be different varieties of apples available. This is a good thing, because it helps you discover new types.

☐ WINGED SEED

2 points

Many trees can have winged seeds, but one of the most popular is a maple tree. Maples have those helicopter-type seeds that you can toss up in the air and watch them spin down a little at a time.

Try to find a couple of different types of winged seeds this fall; if you do, give yourself a couple extra points. Also watch for animals that pick up these seeds and carry them off to stash for winter. This should be worth two points too!

☐ PUMPKIN

1 point

More than 1.5 billion pounds of pumpkins are grown in the United States each year. The states that produce the most are Illinois, Indiana, Ohio, Pennsylvania, and California.

(Illinois takes the top honor, producing about 95 percent of all pumpkins!) Nearly all of these pumpkins are harvested during the month of October.

☐ CHRYSANTHEMUMS

2 points

Chrysanthemums can bloom in summer, but they are most popular in fall. In fact, they're even known as the "favorite flower" for the month of November. In many cultures, the chrysanthemum is a sign of happiness and joy. This flower is actually native to the tropics, and next to the rose, it's one of the most popular and recognized flowers around the world.

My Own Fall Scavenger Hunt Checklist

☐ _____

☐ _____

☐ _____

☐ _____

☐ _____

☐ _____

☐ _____

☐ _____

☐ _____

38 WINTER SCAVENGER HUNT

Winter can have short days and chilly nights, but it's still a really great season to go outside and explore. You just have to be dressed right. Often it seems like there's nothing to do outside during this season, but that's definitely not the case. Take a look at all these great things you should be looking for. Each of these items can be an outing or an experience. Work on this scavenger hunt list a little at a time, and be proud when you've checked everything off.

NUMBER OF ITEMS: 8
TOTAL POINTS POSSIBLE: 16

☐ ICICLE

1 point
Even if you live in a warmer state, there's bound to be an icicle you can find at some point in winter. Look for icicles forming along edges of houses and even from outside mirrors on cars. If your area is going through a particularly cold spell and you have lots of icicles forming, you might even have to knock them down. They can get to be really heavy and may cause damage to your roof or home.

☐ EVERGREEN TREES (3 DIFFERENT TYPES)

3 points

Evergreen trees get their name because they really are green year-round, even in winter. Some people also call evergreens conifers. At first, evergreen trees might look all the same, with long pine needles. But they can actually be quite different from one to the next. Try to get up close to compare the different bark, needles, and other details. You'll start to notice subtle differences, and then it won't be so hard to spot three different types.

☐ SNOW-COVERED PINECONE

3 points

First you have to know where to find pinecones. Then you have to wait for a good snow. Then you need to capture it with a photo. Well, the third one is optional, but a light dusting of snow just sitting on top of a pinecone does make a really good picture. Better yet, try to go outside right after a snowfall so it's really fresh.

☐ SQUIRREL WITH A NUT

3 points

Squirrels gather a lot of nuts in summer
and fall, saving them up to get through
the long days of winter. This one could
be the most challenging on the list,
because now you want to spot a squirrel
with one of those nuts he or she has been saving up. If you can't
quite get this one, try visiting a bird feeder at someone's house
or a nature center. Squirrels will come out to sneak some seed
from the birds.

☐ TREE WITHOUT ANY LEAVES

2 points

At first this might seem easy. After all,
trees drop all their leaves in the fall,
right? Well, not all trees do. But still, it's
kind of a challenge to find a tree that is
100 percent bare. The tree really needs
to have all the leaves gone for it to truly
count. It's not as easy as it sounds once you put these rules into
place, but it's a fun one to try for as you're out on a winter hike.

☐ CHICKADEE

1 point

The chickadee is one of the most common birds in America, and it's especially out and about during winter. You'll often see chickadees at bird feeders, stopping by for something to eat. There are seven different types of chickadees in North America. The most common throughout the country are the black-capped, Carolina, and mountain chickadees. Which one you'll see likely depends on where you live.

☐ FROZEN PUDDLE

1 point

This one should be easy to find, but you might have to go off the beaten path a bit. Look at little shallows at nature centers or at parks that have filled with water and frozen over. This is a good reminder of just how many birds and other animals need water during winter. If you have a backyard where you can regularly provide fresh water or have a heated birdbath, then definitely do. The wildlife will thank you.

☐ RED BARK

2 points

During winter, when things look so dull, bright colors like red can really stand out. Look for a tree or shrub that has red bark to mark this one off your list. One of the most common and popular plants

with red bark is red-twig dogwood, often growing as a shrub. You can see this at most botanical gardens, nature centers, or just growing wild in fields. It's a good plant for wildlife and also a good one to try growing in your own backyard.

My Own Winter Scavenger Hunt Checklist

☐ _____

☐ _____

☐ _____

☐ _____

☐ _____

☐ _____

☐ _____

☐ _____

☐ _____

Chapter 8

GO AT THE RIGHT TIME

Have you ever heard the phrase "You were at the right place at the right time"? This is what you want to happen as you work on the scavenger hunts in this chapter. These really do have a lot to do with timing and being somewhere in the right moment. As you work on these, really pay attention to little details during the time of day recommended for each one. How does one part of the day differ from the next? As you notice things like lighting and the overall mood of being outside, it really makes you aware of the natural world in a whole new way.

39 EARLY MORNING SCAVENGER HUNT

If you're a morning person, you know how amazing the early hours can be. It's so quiet and calm. When you go out to enjoy the day, it really feels like you are waking up with the world around you. This scavenger hunt is best to do as early in the day as possible. You'll have the best chance of crossing everything off your list this way.

NUMBER OF ITEMS: 8
TOTAL POINTS POSSIBLE: 18

☐ EPIC SUNRISE

2 points

Getting up before the sun is not an easy thing to do, especially during summer, when the days are longer than the nights. However, it's one of those things you truly have to experience in person.

To get up before the sunrise, look up the time of sunrise in your area. Then arrive at least 15 to 20 minutes before (30 would be best). This way you'll be able to see how the sky and colors change as sun starts lifting up over the horizon.

☐ SOMETHING WITH DEW

2 points

It doesn't have to rain in order to see dew in the morning. Dew is actually a collection of water drops caused by condensation. Dew forms because objects that have heated up during the day from the sun start to lose that heat (and therefore moisture) at night. So if you're up early in the morning, you'll see that moisture collecting as dew. It's especially cool to see dew hanging from a flower. Grab your camera, because this can be a really great photo moment.

☐ BABY ANIMAL

3 points

As you're out and about in the morning, be aware of your surrounding and watch for animals out exploring. Early morning is the perfect time to catch a little bunny rabbit, bird, or chipmunk, which often get up with the sun to start their day. If you see an adult animal with the baby, give yourself two extra points. And if you see multiple babies, give yourself an extra point for each one you see! If you find this one challenging, try going to a pond or open body of water. This will definitely increase your chances, because mama ducks and geese like to take their babies for a morning swim.

☐ FLOWERS CURLED UP

2 points

Many flowers curl up at night, rolling into a little ball of petals. Then when the sun comes out, they start to uncurl as they reach toward the rays in the sky. Not all flowers do this, so you have to be on the lookout for those that do. Don't try to touch or open the flowers at all. Just enjoy the cool moment and maybe snap a picture when you see it. Try to see how many different plants you can spot that have curled-up flowers.

☐ BUG CRAWLING

2 points

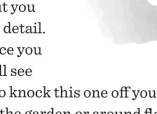

This one should be pretty easy, but you still have to pay close attention to detail. Bugs tend to go unnoticed, but once you start really looking for them, you'll see them all the time. One good way to knock this one off your list is to keep an eye out when you're in the garden or around flowers. Bugs love visiting plants in the early hours before it gets too hot. You can also try to knock this one out around a lake or pond.

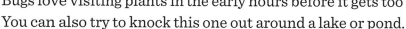

☐ BIRD CHIRPING

2 points

You will probably hear this one before you see it, but to really make it count, you should challenge yourself to find the bird. Listen closely and follow the sound. Can you see the bird? Can you tell what it is? Many say the American robin is one of the first birds to sing in the morning, but it could really be any species. If you can hear multiple bird species chirping (and see them too), give yourself an extra point.

☐ MOON GOING TO BED

3 points

If you get up early enough (like when you go to see the sunrise), you might be able to see the moon going to bed at the same time. To increase your chances of knocking this one off your list, be sure to wake up early and go out on a really clear night. You won't be able to see the moon if it's all cloudy.

☐ FOG

2 points

Fog and dew are definitely related. Fog forms because of a change in temperature and moisture in the air. To cross this one off your list and see a cool sight at the same time, go to a lake, pond, or big body of water. You'll be sure to see fog in the early morning hours.

My Own Early Morning Scavenger Hunt Checklist

☐ _____

☐ _____

☐ _____

☐ _____

☐ _____

☐ _____

☐ _____

☐ _____

40 AFTERNOON SCAVENGER HUNT

Afternoons seem to fly by, especially when you're outside. You can work on this scavenger hunt just about anywhere, because there are a lot of different ways you can check off the items. Most of them are left up to your interpretation, which will really challenge you to think in creative ways. This is also a good scavenger hunt to turn into a photo challenge. Break up into two teams and take pictures as you go. When you're both done, trade photos of what you saw.

NUMBER OF ITEMS: 8
TOTAL POINTS POSSIBLE: 13

☐ SOMETHING SMOOTH
1 point

SMOOTH

Your something smooth can really be anything, but here's a challenge you can take on as a family or a group. Go to a lake or river and challenge everyone to find the smoothest rock possible. Set a timer for about 5 or 10 minutes, and GO! Once the time is up, have everyone close their eyes and feel each rock to see which one is smoothest. You want to do this as a blind test so that you don't know whose rock is whose.

☐ SOMETHING SHINY

2 points

What exactly is shiny in nature? Some rocks are shiny. Metals are shiny. You might even find shiny leaves or flowers if you locate the right types. Go out and try to find the shiniest thing possible while

on a hike or nature walk. If you are able to collect it, you should. If not, take a picture so you can compare it later on. Try to gather up multiple shiny objects so you can see which one has the most shine at the end.

☐ SOMETHING SOFT

2 points

When you really look at what's around you, it's easy to find things that are soft. Check out the flowers and plants around you and gently touch their leaves. Look for grass that is soft and gentle, not

spiky or hard. If it has rained recently, you might find that the ground or soil is soft too. You can do this challenge anywhere, but it's especially fun to try it in your own backyard.

☐ SOMETHING ROUGH

1 point

Many items in the soft category can also feel rough. Plants or flowers might have a rough texture. Grass or the ground might also be rough. Trees are another rough item in nature. Be careful as you're exploring plants—you don't want to grab something that has thorns and will poke you. But do gently feel the textures around you as you explore.

☐ SOMETHING FUZZY

3 points

Right away, you might be thinking of a fuzzy animal, right? Well, since you probably shouldn't pick up animals in the wild, you might have to be creative with this one. (Although if you see a fuzzy animal—like a bunny or a squirrel with a fluffy tail—this should count.) Also look for fuzzy objects that float through the air, moved from one place to the next by the wind. Fuzzy items tend to be lightweight, so this is a good one to be on the lookout for when you're out for a walk.

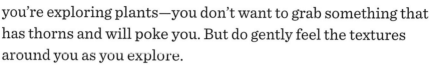

☐ SOMETHING COLORFUL

2 points

The colors of nature can be bright, bold, and beautiful. You can find rich reds in flowers and bright blues in waters. But have you tried to find something in nature that has many colors? For this scavenger hunt item, look for something that is very colorful, mixing different hues. This could include the bark of a tree, a rock, or a flower that has multiple colors. Try to find something with as many colors as possible.

☐ SOMETHING TINY

1 point

It seems easy at first, right? In some ways it is. There are plenty of tiny things you can find in nature. However, this should be one where you really challenge yourself. What is the tiniest thing you can find? Is it smaller than an apple? Can you find something even smaller than a quarter? How about smaller than a grain of rice? Find the tiniest thing possible yourself—or turn it into a family challenge.

☐ SOMETHING HEAVY

1 point

The obvious item here is a tree or a rock—both are things in nature that are big and heavy. However, that's almost too easy. Try to make this one even more challenging by not choosing one of those items. Or if you do go for a tree or a rock, try to make it a unique or really cool one. This will really get you looking at your surroundings in a different way.

My Own Afternoon Scavenger Hunt Checklist

☐ _____

☐ _____

☐ _____

☐ _____

☐ _____

☐ _____

☐ _____

☐ _____

☐ _____

⚲ 41 DUSK SCAVENGER HUNT

Do you like to make the most of your day? If you do, then you already know that dusk is a great part of the day to see and experience nature. If you're dealing with hot temperatures, it tends to be a cooler part of the day. It's also a good time for animal activity, as those who were out during the day go in and those who were sleeping during the day come out.

NUMBER OF ITEMS: 8
TOTAL POINTS POSSIBLE: 15

☐ BAT

3 points

Bats have a special skill called echolocation. They make noise and wait for the sound to echo back at them. If the echo is really strong and close, they'll know there is an object close, and they need to find a different way. When they can finally make sound and it doesn't echo (or the echo is really far), they know it's clear ahead of them and they can move forward.

EPIC SUNSET

2 points

If you want to see the most epic sunset, there are a few tips you should keep in mind. First of all, you want a clear day. It's nice to have a few clouds in the sky, but you don't want it to be super cloudy. Next, find a good spot that has a beautiful view of where the sun is going down. Since you know the sun sets in the west, try to find a spot that is high up, looking into the west or looking out toward water. Finally, be sure to arrive at least half an hour before sunset and stay at least 15 minutes after to see all the great colors and enjoy a truly epic experience.

THE FIRST STAR

2 points

The first star is not always the brightest star, but it almost always shows up at dusk. This is such a fun challenge to share with family or friends. See who can spot the first star. When you do, be sure to make a wish! Here's a little rhyme you can say when you find the first star: "Star light, star bright—first star I see tonight. I wish I may, I wish I might, have this wish I wish tonight."

☐ FIREFLY

2 points

Fireflies glow because of a special animal
power called bioluminescence. This
basically means they can generate their
own light. Fireflies can have lights that
are green, yellow, or orange. If you see
a firefly at dusk, take a really good look
at it. Then try to spot it during the day
as an extra challenge. Yes, these insects
are most active at night, but they can be out in the daytime too.
They just might look a little different to you.

☐ TOAD

1 point

You know how they say toads can give
you warts? This is not true! It's a myth,
so be sure to tell others. The bumps
on toads do serve a purpose, though.
They are glands that can be poisonous
to predators. This is a really cool defense mechanism. If
something tries to eat a toad, it can give off a foul taste that
makes the predator drop the toad right there!

☐ RABBIT

1 point

Have you ever noticed a rabbit's eyes? If not, take a close look the next time you see a bunny hopping around. Rabbits' eyes are really more on the side of their heads. This is pretty cool because it allows them to see all around. This is a great thing for keeping an eye out for predators. It helps them see them sooner and try to get away.

☐ PURPLE SKY

3 points

The color of the sky can be a fascinating thing. From red, pink, and purple, it can be really cool to see a bright and colorful sky as the sun goes down. It's hard to predict just what color you might get—a lot of things are factored into this, like the angle of the sun, the sunlight, and how it all hits the atmosphere. But a purple sky can be unique, so you get three points for this!

☐ SHADOW

1 point

There's a magical time of day when the shadows look really cool—and that's dusk. You can really spot a shadow any time of the day, but try to go out and see how they look just before dark. Look for shadows from trees, flowers, and even yourself. Then try to capture a cool shadow in a picture!

My Own Dusk Scavenger Hunt Checklist

☐ _____

☐ _____

☐ _____

☐ _____

☐ _____

☐ _____

☐ _____

☐ _____

42 NIGHTTIME SCAVENGER HUNT

Just because it's dark out doesn't mean there aren't plenty of things to see. This isn't an easy scavenger hunt to conquer, but it's worth it! Going on a nighttime scavenger hunt can be a great adventure to have as a family. Grab a flashlight and pack a snack, because there are some cool things to find. Be sure to add your own things to the list as well.

NUMBER OF ITEMS: 10
TOTAL POINTS POSSIBLE: 24

☐ FULL MOON

2 points

If you look up the full moon schedule online, this one should be easy to cross off your list. Now it still needs to be a clear night in order to get a good view. But go ahead and see when the next full moon is, and then put it on your calendar. This will help you remember to go and check it out.

☐ OWL

3 points

Owls come out at night for the main purpose of hunting. They are nocturnal animals and will try to hunt other nocturnal animals in the evening. They use their large, sharp talons as their tool

for hunting. As they dive down, often without making a sound, they can scoop up prey in just a couple of seconds.

☐ NIGHTCRAWLER

2 points

Nightcrawlers (aka earthworms) can be spotted any time of day, but it's especially cool to try to find one at night. They do come out in the evening, and there's a good reason why. They dry out

easily, so they move around at night when it's cooler. If you have trouble with this one, try digging in the soil of a garden. You're sure to find a nightcrawler then.

☐ MOONFLOWER

3 points

Moonflowers are beautiful white flowers that only bloom at night. This makes them really popular with moths, since these insects mostly come out at night too. If you see a moonflower, be a

little cautious around it. They are very poisonous, so you want to look but not touch.

☐ OPOSSUM OR RACCOON

2 points

Both opossums and raccoons are active at night, so if you see either one, you get to cross it off the list. A lot of people don't like opossums because they aren't the cutest animal out there, but they are actually really cool. They have pouches just like kangaroos, making them part of a group of mammals called marsupials. They eat a lot of ticks, which is a good thing for you.

☐ MILKY WAY

3 points

It's hard to explain the Milky Way—you really have to see it. There are so many stars in one area in the Milky Way that it appears like a haze across the sky. In order to see it, you need to be outside on a clear night and in a remoter area—away from the bright lights of a city. You want it to be dark too, so it's best to try to see the Milky Way during a new moon, not a full moon. When you finally get to see this one, it will take your breath away.

☐ NORTH STAR

2 points

The North Star, also called Polaris, is really cool because it's one of the only stars that doesn't seem to shift its place in the sky. It has a position relative to the Earth's axis, so while other stars appear to move and rise and set during the night and over seasons, the North Star sits in one spot. A lot of people think the North Star is the brightest star in the sky, but that's not true. It only ranks forty-sixth in brightness overall.

☐ SHOOTING STAR

3 points

A shooting star is actually a burning meteor or piece of meteor as it flies through the sky at night. You can see more shooting stars during periodic meteor showers. Do a web search for upcoming meteor showers in your area to know when to go out to look. When you see a shooting star, you'll definitely want to pause for a moment and make a wish. It's tradition, and it's a good one to keep going.

☐ CRICKET

2 points

This fact might gross you out a bit, but it's still cool. Many people eat crickets all over the world. In fact, some people use crickets to make things like cricket flour, which they use in place of regular flour when baking. Even though it might make your nose scrunch up when you think about eating these bugs, they can actually be really good for you. They can also be a good source of protein, and this is great for parts of the world that have limited food resources.

☐ MOTH

2 points

Most (but not all) moths are nocturnal and are most active at night. Moths and butterflies are different, but sometimes it can be hard to tell how. One of the easiest ways is to look at how it's resting. A moth often rests with its wings open, while a butterfly rests with its wings closed. If you want to see moths, leave your back porch light on at night. This is definitely a way to attract moths to your backyard and get a closer look.

My Own Nighttime
Scavenger Hunt Checklist

- [ ] _____
- [ ] _____
- [ ] _____
- [ ] _____
- [ ] _____
- [ ] _____
- [ ] _____
- [ ] _____
- [ ] _____

ABOUT THE AUTHOR

Stacy Tornio is the author of more than fifteen books for families and kids, including a book with her son, Jack, *101 Outdoor Adventures to Have Before You Grow Up* (FalconGuides). This book was a recipient of a National Outdoor Book Award in 2019. She's also written books on gardening, animals, the national parks, and several titles for the National Wildlife Federation's Ranger Rick brand.

Stacy runs the website DestinationNature.com, which has free printables and resources for kids and parents. She is also the director of content for the nonprofit Let Grow. Let Grow promotes childhood independence and believes it's a critical part of growing up.

Stacy lives in Milwaukee, Wisconsin, with her two kids, and they've done a lot of scavenger hunts over the years.